WITHDRAWN

Writing the Critical Essay

Marijuana

An OPPOSING VIEWPOINTS® Guide

Writing the Critical Essay

Marijuana

An OPPOSING VIEWPOINTS® Guide

Other books in the Writing the Critical Essay series are:

Writing the Critical Essay

Marijuana

An OPPOSING VIEWPOINTS® Guide

Louise I. Gerdes, *Book Editor*

Christine Nasso, *Publisher*
Elizabeth Des Chenes, *Managing Editor*

OPPOSING
VIEWPOINTS®
SERIES

GREENHAVEN PRESS
An imprint of Thomson Gale, a part of The Thomson Corporation

Detroit • New York • San Francisco • New Haven, Conn. • Waterville, Maine • London

© 2007 Thomson Gale, a part of The Thomson Corporation.

Thomson and Star Logo are trademarks and Gale and Greenhaven Press are registered trademarks used herein under license.

For more information, contact:
Greenhaven Press
27500 Drake Rd.
Farmington Hills, MI 48331-3535
Or you can visit our Internet site at http://www.gale.com

ALL RIGHTS RESERVED.
No part of this work covered by the copyright hereon may be reproduced or used in any form or by any means—graphic, electronic, or mechanical, including photocopying, recording, taping, Web distribution or information storage retrieval systems—without the written permission of the publisher.

Articles in Greenhaven Press anthologies are often edited for length to meet page requirements. In addition, original titles of these works are changed to clearly present the main thesis and to explicitly indicate the author's opinion. Every effort is made to ensure that Greenhaven Press accurately reflects the original intent of the authors.

Every effort has been made to trace the owners of copyrighted material.

LIBRARY OF CONGRESS CATALOGING-IN-PUBLICATION DATA

Marijuana / Louise I. Gerdes, book editor.
   p. cm. — (Writing the critical essay)
 Includes bibliographical references and index.
 ISBN-13: 978-0-7377-3583-3 (alk. paper)
 ISBN-10: 0-7377-3583-X (alk. paper)
 1. Marijuana—Government policy. 2. Marijuana—Social aspects. I. Gerdes,
Louise I., 1953–
 HV5822.M3M2665 2007
 616.86'35—dc22

                                                    2006031173

Printed in the United States of America

CONTENTS

Examining the state of writing and how it is taught in the United States was the official purpose of the National Commission on Writing in America's Schools and Colleges. The commission, made up of teachers, school administrators, business leaders, and college and university presidents, released its first report in 2003. "Despite the best efforts of many educators," commissioners argued, "writing has not received the full attention it deserves." Among the findings of the commission was that most fourth-grade students spent less than three hours a week writing, that three-quarters of high school seniors never receive a writing assignment in their history or social studies classes, and that more than 50 percent of first-year students in college have problems writing error-free papers. The commission called for a "cultural sea change" that would increase the emphasis on writing for both elementary and secondary schools. These conclusions have made some educators realize that writing must be emphasized in the curriculum. As colleges are demanding an ever-higher level of writing proficiency from incoming students, schools must respond by making students more competent writers. In response to these concerns, the SAT, an influential standardized test used for college admissions, required an essay for the first time in 2005.

Books in the Writing the Critical Essay: An Opposing Viewpoints Guide series use the patented Opposing Viewpoints format to help students learn to organize ideas and arguments and to write essays using common critical writing techniques. Each book in the series focuses on a particular type of essay writing—including expository, persuasive, descriptive, and narrative—that students learn while being taught both the five-paragraph essay as well as longer pieces of writing that have an opinionated focus. These guides include everything necessary to help students research, outline, draft, edit, and ultimately write successful essays across the curriculum, including essays for the SAT.

Using Opposing Viewpoints

This series is inspired by and builds upon Greenhaven Press's acclaimed Opposing Viewpoints series. As in the parent series, each book in the Writing the Critical Essay series focuses on a timely and controversial social issue that provides lots of opportunities for creating thought-provoking essays. The first section of each volume begins with a brief introductory essay that provides context for the opposing viewpoints that follow. These articles are chosen for their accessibility and clearly stated views. The thesis of each article is made explicit in the article's title and is accentuated by its pairing with an opposing or alternative view. These essays are both models of persuasive writing techniques and valuable research material that students can mine to write their own informed essays. Guided reading and discussion questions help lead students to key ideas and writing techniques presented in the selections.

The second section of each book begins with a preface discussing the format of the essays and examining characteristics of the featured essay type. Model five-paragraph and longer essays then demonstrate that essay type. The essays are annotated so that key writing elements and techniques are pointed out to the student. Sequential, step-by-step exercises help students construct and refine thesis statements; organize material into outlines; analyze and try out writing techniques; write transitions, introductions, and conclusions; and incorporate quotations and other researched material. Ultimately, students construct their own compositions using the designated essay type.

The third section of each volume provides additional research material and writing prompts to help the student. Additional facts about the topic of the book serve as a convenient source of supporting material for essays. Other features help students go beyond the book for their research. Like other Greenhaven Press books, each book in the Writing the Critical Essay series includes bibliographic listings of relevant periodical articles, books, Web sites, and organizations to contact.

Writing the Critical Essay: An Opposing Viewpoints Guide will help students master essay techniques that can be used in any discipline.

Background to Controversy: Marijuana and Medicine

Marijuana has been used as a medicine, an intoxicant, and a practical commodity for centuries. In fact, the hemp plant, from which marijuana is derived, was one of the first crops grown by colonists who arrived on America's shores in the 1600s. Hemp could be used to make rope, paper, and building materials. The first Levi Strauss jeans were made from hemp. In the early twentieth century, Mexican immigrants introduced marijuana as an intoxicant in the United States, but not until the 1930s did Americans become concerned about the potential dangers of the drug. Even at that time, however, the drug's dangers were hotly disputed. Since then, attitudes toward the drug and its dangers have waxed and waned.

The U.S. federal government classifies marijuana as a Schedule I drug, believing it to be dangerous and addictive with no medicinal value. Therefore marijuana is currently illegal at the federal level for any use, recreational or medical. Nevertheless, millions of Americans use marijuana and millions more have at one point tried the drug. In addition, despite the federal government's prohibition of marijuana, more than 10 states have enacted laws allowing its use as medicine. Why do so many Americans use a drug that the government claims is so dangerous? Why have some states enacted laws allowing the use of marijuana as medicine despite the government's position that it has no medical value? The answers to these questions represent the cornerstone controversy in the marijuana debate.

An Issue of Health

Those who see marijuana as a threat to public health believe it is a dangerous, addictive drug. The National Institute on

States that Have Legalized Medical Marijuana

Alaska, California, Colorado, Hawaii, Maine, Montana, Nevada, Oregon, Rhode Island, Vermont, and Washington have legalized medical marijuana.

Drug Abuse (NIDA), part of the U.S. Department of Health and Human Services, claims that marijuana use impairs memory, damages the lungs, weakens the immune system, reduces motivation, and leads to addiction and the use of other dangerous drugs. Indeed, in 2004 there were 215,665 emergency room visits relating to marijuana, and hundreds of thousands of people seek treatment every year for marijuana abuse and addiction. Furthermore, some studies endorsed by the American Psychiatric Association and the White House Office of National Drug Control Policy (ONDCP) have shown that marijuana can lead to depression, suicidal tendencies, and even mental disorders such as schizophrenia. According to John P. Walters, the director of the ONDCP, "There are laws against marijuana because marijuana is harmful. With every year that passes, medical research discovers greater dangers from smoking it, from links to serious mental illness to the risk of cancer."[1]

But others believe that marijuana is a relatively harmless drug with useful medicinal properties. A 1999 study from Johns Hopkins University found, for example, that although marijuana damages a user's cognitive and memory functions while high, they are not permanently or irreversibly impaired. Furthermore, compared with legal substances such as alcohol and tobacco, the health risks of marijuana seem minimal. For instance, the group National Organization for the Reform of Marijuana Laws (NORML) reports that no one has ever died from an overdose of marijuana, while hundreds of thousands die each year from tobacco- and alcohol-related causes. There are also far fewer traffic accidents related to marijuana than to alcohol. Says NORML analyst Paul Armentano, "Almost all drugs—including those that are legal—pose greater threats to individual health and/or society than does marijuana."[2]

But even if there are some health risks from using marijuana, supporters and users of medical marijuana believe that such risks can be no worse than the health problems they already have. If marijuana helps patients overcome nausea, tolerate food and water, and relieve physical pain, most are unconcerned if it impairs their memory or even puts them at risk for lung damage. Indeed, in the states that have legalized it, medical marijuana has improved the lives of many seriously ill patients. In addition to relieving chronic pain, the drug has for many patients alleviated the side effects that accompany treatment for cancer or the symptoms of other diseases. One such patient is Angel Raich, who suffers from "wasting syndrome" in which she cannot eat or drink. Raich has taken medical marijuana since 1997 to stimulate her appetite so she is able to eat enough to sustain herself. "I don't know how to explain it," said Raich. "I just can't swallow without cannabis."[3]

An Issue of States' Rights

Part of the medical marijuana debate that is especially confusing is that despite being categorized as an illegal substance on the federal level, individual states have been allowed to make their own laws about marijuana. Since 1996, eleven states have legalized medical marijuana use: Alaska, California, Colorado, Hawaii, Maine, Montana, Nevada, Oregon, Rhode Island, Vermont, and Washington. But the safety of legalized medical marijuana in those states is far from assured. In fact, the federal government regularly sends armed squads of federal agents into California to break up its medical marijuana cooperatives there—one such raid occurred on September 5, 2002, when DEA agents raided the Wo/Men's Alliance for Medical Marijuana (WAMM) cooperative in Santa Cruz. While some see these raids as legitimate drug busts, others view them as a violation of states' rights, the right of states protected by the Tenth Amendment which enables them to make their own laws regarding matters that are not expressly discussed in the Constitution.

To determine the matter, the question of whether states or the federal government have the right to regulate medical marijuana has been considered in a sequence of court cases. The most recent Supreme Court decision came on June 6, 2005. By a vote of 6 to 3 in a case called *Raich v. Gonzales*, the Court ruled that the federal government has a right to overturn state laws and prohibit the use of medical marijuana. But just how far the federal government will go in acting on its power, especially in the face of state voters who staunchly stand by their initiatives, remains to be seen.

The complicated debate over medical marijuana is unlikely to wane anytime soon. Therefore, understanding the many issues of the debate, and determining what marijuana policies will best serve the American people, is an important task. To this end, *Writing the Critical Essay: An Opposing Viewpoints Guide: Marijuana* exposes readers to the basic arguments made about marijuana and encourages them to develop their own opinions on whether or not marijuana is harmful, should be legal, or should be considered medicine. Through skill-building exercises and thoughtful discussion questions, students will articulate their own thoughts about marijuana and develop tools to craft their own essays on the subject.

Notes

1. John P. Walters, "No Surrender: The Drug War Saves Lives," *National Review*, September 27, 2004.

2. Paul Armentano, "The 2005 NORML Truth Report," National Organization for the Reform of Marijuana Laws, July 21, 2005.

3. Quoted in Charles Lane, "A Defeat for Users of Medical Marijuana," *Washington Post*, June 7, 2005.

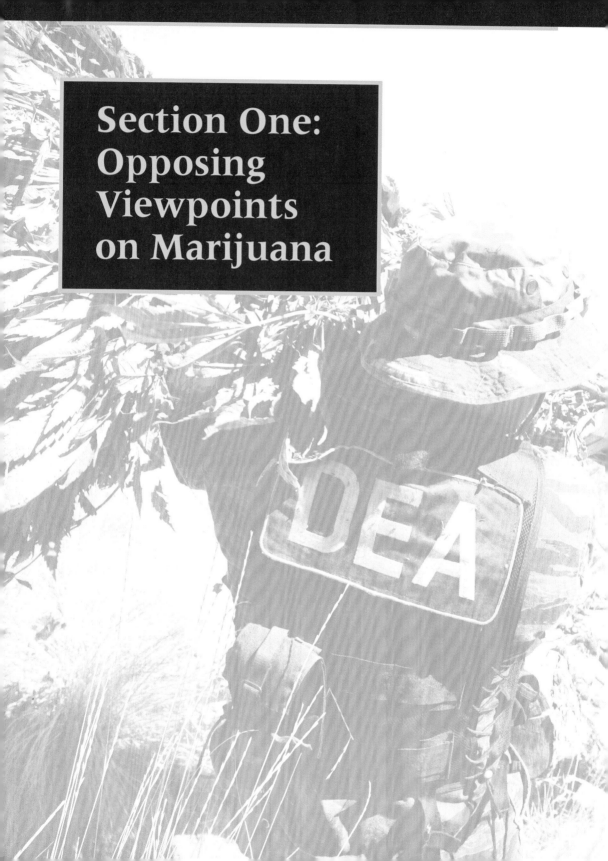

Section One: Opposing Viewpoints on Marijuana

Marijuana Is a Dangerous Drug

Joseph V. Amodio

In the following essay Joseph V. Amodio argues that marijuana is a dangerous drug with harmful, long-lasting effects. Amodio claims that marijuana impairs memory, reaction time, and motivation. Those who smoke marijuana, he claims, may lose interest in school and sports, while some users become more likely to use harder drugs such as heroin.

Amodio is a freelance writer who writes on current issues for magazines such as *Current Health 2*.

Consider the following questions:

1. According to the author, what are some of the different reactions people have to marijuana?
2. What happened to the reaction time of pilots who smoked marijuana in one study cited by Amodio?
3. In Amodio's opinion, why do many users become addicted to marijuana?

L ate one evening in the fall of 2004, doctors wheeled a 17-year-old girl into the emergency room at the Stanford University Medical Center in California. The girl was suffering from multiple injuries sustained when the car she was driving flipped over. The teen survived, but another girl, who'd been sitting in the passenger seat, did not. At the hospital, doctors tested the driver's blood for toxins or drugs. The test results showed that the driver had smoked marijuana, or pot, before the crash.

Joseph V. Amodio, "Why Pot Is Not Cool: How Marijuana Messes with Your Brain and Body," *Current Health* 2, Vol. 31, March, 2005, pp. 11-13. Reproduced by permission.

"She was a nice kid who really, really messed up," said Kelly Murphy, one of the doctors on call that night. "It's sad. She was only 17, and now she faces charges of motor-vehicle homicide, in addition to the guilt of killing someone—her best friend."

The Problem with Pot

Many people believe marijuana is harmless because people can't die from it. But that's not the whole truth, says Scott Teitelbaum, a physician and the medical director of the Florida Recovery Center, a drug abuse facility in Gainesville. People can't overdose on pot, as they can on heroin, he admits. And a pot user won't suddenly suffer a heart attack, which sometimes happens to people who use cocaine.

But marijuana's effects can sneak up on an unsuspecting user. Slowly, quietly, without the user's even noticing, the frequent use of pot can impair brain activity, physical coordination, and—worst of all—motivation to try new things, make friends, do schoolwork, or seek help if drug use is getting out of control. "Marijuana is insidious," said Teitelbaum.

The drug, which is also known as weed or reefer, is usually chopped up and smoked like a cigarette, called a joint. Marijuana contains a strong chemical called THC [tetrahydrocannabinol]. THC can make people feel relaxed and can distract them from problems. But some people who smoke marijuana feel nothing; others may feel frightened or nervous. The relaxed feeling, also known as a high, lasts only a few hours, but the drug remains in the body for days and can affect users even when they don't feel high, or stoned.

A Multitude of Negative Effects

Marijuana stifles motivation; retards the maturation process; adversely affects short term memory and one's ability to learn; enhances the onset of mental illness; is very high in cancer causing agents; adversely affects reproductive organs and has a multitude of other negative physiological effects.

Roger Morgan, DAMMADD.org, March 30, 2005. www.dammadd.org.

The number of emergency room visits in which marijuana use was mentioned rose to nearly 120,000 in 2002, triple the number in 1994.

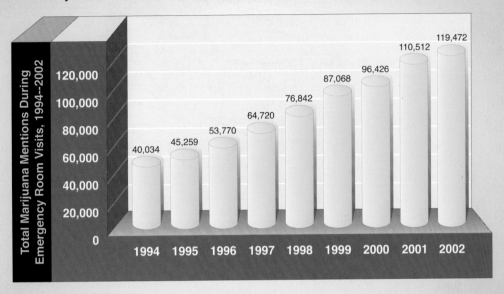

Source: Substance Abuse and Mental Health Services Administration, SAMHSA News, 2003.

Long-Lasting Effects

"An interesting study was done with airline pilots," Teitelbaum noted. In 1985, scientists gave pilots a small amount of marijuana and then tested their reaction time and abilities as they operated a computer program designed to simulate flying and landing a plane. "When the pilots were stoned, they knew they were messing up the test and they all did terribly," said Teitelbaum. Twenty-four hours later, when the pilots believed they were fine, they took the test again—and still did poorly.

According to Teitelbaum, marijuana can affect how people think and what they do "for hours, maybe even days after." And it's not just reaction time that's impaired by pot. Memory, decision making, even the ability to find the right words when speaking, can be affected. That may explain why a student who gets high on the weekend can

"Wish I could!"

Jeliffe, www.cartoonstock.com. © Ray Jeliffe. Reproduced by permission.

still end up stumbling through a class presentation in the middle of the following week.

Stronger than Ever

Experts on drug abuse report that marijuana is stronger today than ever before. That's because the plants contain more THC than they did in the past. Pot can be up to five times as potent as it was in the 1970s, making its use by today's kids especially dangerous. "Playing with marijuana is like playing with fire," said Joseph Califano Jr., the chairman and president of the National Center on Addiction and Substance Abuse at Columbia University in New York City.

Teens who use pot may find themselves missing out on life. "A regular marijuana user is less likely to enjoy reading or studying or playing sports than someone who doesn't use drugs," said Mark Gold, a professor at the University of Florida in Gainesville. That is one reason many users may become addicted. The sense of being high tricks the brain into thinking that everything else seems dull.

From Bad to Worse

Although some kids smoke pot without becoming addicted, many others get hooked and find it hard to stop. Even worse, the high that users crave becomes harder to achieve, so they must smoke more pot or take more dangerous drugs to attain it. Research shows that most cocaine and heroin addicts, for example, started out smoking pot. That's why doctors call marijuana a gateway drug.

The reality is, no one can predict how he or she will react until passing through that "gate." Yet experts know that nearly a quarter million Americans enter drug treatment programs each year—and their number-one problem is pot.

Analyze the essay:

1. The author begins his essay with the tragic story of a young girl who flipped her car under the influence of marijuana. Do you think this is an effective way to begin an essay? Explain your reasoning.

2. In this essay Amodio claims that marijuana is a dangerous drug. In the following essay Maia Szalavitz argues that the dangers of marijuana have been exaggerated. After reading both essays, with which author do you agree? What pieces of evidence helped you form your opinion?

The Dangers of Marijuana Are Exaggerated

Maia Szalavitz

In the following viewpoint author Maia Szalavitz argues that marijuana is not as dangerous as antidrug agencies would have people believe. She discusses one advertisement published by the government that exaggerated the link between marijuana and mental illness. Furthermore, Szalavitz says that the government has overstated both the potency and effects of marijuana. She warns that exaggerating the dangers of marijuana can damage the credibility of antidrug efforts because teens will be reluctant to believe warnings about drugs that are much more dangerous than marijuana.

Szalavitz is the author of *Tough Love America: How the 'Troubled Teen' Industry Cons Parents and Hurts Kids*. Her work has appeared in newspapers such as the *Chicago Sun-Times*, from which this viewpoint was taken.

Consider the following questions:

1. What is one piece of evidence used by Szalavitz to argue that marijuana does not cause schizophrenia?
2. According to the author, are today's marijuana users smoking stronger pot than previous generations of users?
3. What were the results of a June 2005 University of Southern California study about marijuana and depression, as reported by Szalavitz?

Maia Szalavitz, "The New Reefer Madness," *Chicago Sun-Times*, October 2, 2005, p. 1. Copyright © Chicago Sun-Times. Reprinted by permission of the author.

Parents who read the *New York Times* or *Newsweek* [in summer 2005 issues] could be forgiven for freaking out when they came across a full-page ad warning them about the effects of marijuana on their teenagers. If the kids were off somewhere sparking up a joint, the federally funded message seemed to say, they were at risk for severe mental illness. Were those parents hallucinating, or was Reefer Madness, long since debunked, suddenly a real problem to be reckoned with?

Alarmist Ads About Marijuana

The latest salvo in the never-ending war on drugs, the ads, which also ran in magazines such as the *Nation* and the *National Review,* bore a stark warning. Under the headline "Marijuana and Your Teen's Mental Health," the bold-faced subhead announced: "Depression. Suicidal Thoughts. Schizophrenia."

"If you have outdated perceptions about marijuana, you might be putting your teen at risk," the text went on. It warned that "young people who use marijuana weekly have double the risk of depression later in life" and that "marijuana use in some teens has been linked to increased risk for schizophrenia." It followed with the sneering question, "Still think marijuana's no big deal?"

The rhetoric is alarming. But the research data used to support the ad campaign is hazy at best. Though carefully worded, the campaign blurs the key scientific distinction between correlation and causation. The ad uses some correlations between marijuana use and mental illness to imply that the drug can cause madness and depression. Yet these conclusions are unproven by current research. And several leading researchers are highly skeptical of them.

The Use of Scare Tactics

Scare tactics in the war on drugs have been around at least since the time of Harry J. Anslinger, the federal drug warrior of the 1930s famed for his ludicrous pronouncements

Harry J. Anslinger, the federal drug warrior of the 1930s, was famous for his antidrug scare tactics.

about the dangers of marijuana. But they're widely regarded as ineffective in deterring teen drug use. In fact, some research suggests they may actually increase experimentation. If anything, experts say, the latest ad campaign's overblown claims could damage credibility with teens, undermining warnings about other, more dangerous illicit substances. With medical marijuana a matter of renewed national debate, and with evidence emerging that there may be no connection between marijuana and lung cancer—a key strike against the drug's use in the past—the government's new campaign smacks more of desperation than science. . . .

Unconvincing Science and Weak Connections

Leading experts in psychiatric epidemiology are far from convinced about causal connections between marijuana and serious mental illness. One key problem, they say, is that it's very difficult to determine if pot smoking predisposes people to schizophrenia, if early symptoms of schizophrenia predispose people to smoking pot, or if some third factor causes some people to be more vulnerable to both.

In [a] Swedish study, for example, when factors already known to increase risk for schizophrenia were removed, such as a childhood history of disturbed behavior, the connection between marijuana use and risk for the disease was substantially reduced. Just one or two additional unknown influences could potentially wipe out the

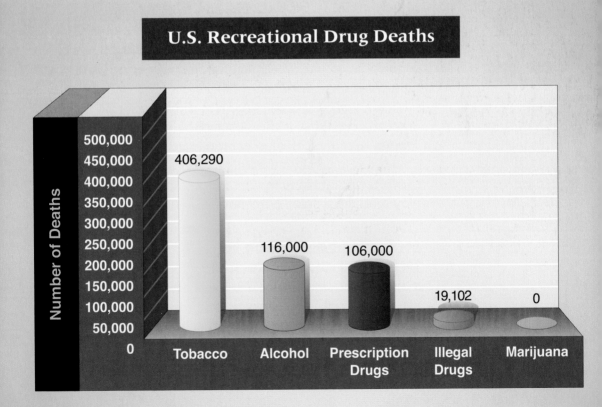

Source: Michael Hess, US Drug War FAQlet, 2002. http://bbsnews.net.

apparent marijuana-schizophrenia link, according to Dr. William Carpenter, a professor of psychiatry and pharmacology at the University of Maryland. Carpenter noted in a letter published in the *British Journal of Psychiatry* in October 2004 that the same genes that predispose someone to schizophrenia might also predispose them to substance abuse, but that drug use might start earlier simply because many people start using drugs in their teen years, while schizophrenia most commonly begins in the early 20s.

Perhaps the strongest piece of evidence to cast doubt on a causal connection between marijuana and schizophrenia is a long flat-line trend in the disease. While marijuana use rose from virtually nil in the 1940s and '50s to a peak period of use in 1979—when about 60 percent of high school seniors had tried it—schizophrenia rates remained virtually constant over those decades. The same remains true today. One percent or fewer people have schizophrenia, a rate consistent among populations around the world. This is in stark contrast to studies linking tobacco smoking with lung cancer, in which increases in tobacco use were accompanied by rising rates of lung cancer.

"If anything, the studies seem to show a possible decline in schizophrenia from the '40s and the '50s," says Dr. Alan Brown, a professor of psychiatry and epidemiology at Columbia University. "If marijuana does have a causal role in schizophrenia, and that's still questionable, it may only play a role in a small percent of cases." . . .

More Exaggerations

The campaign also declares that today's pot is more potent than the pot smoked by previous generations, implying heightened risk. Fine sinsemilla [a highly potent form of marijuana] may seem more prevalent than ditchweed nowadays, but there is debate over whether today's average smoker is puffing on stronger stuff than the average stoner of the 1970s, as Daniel Forbes detailed in *Slate*.

Because today's marijuana is more potent than in the past, some say there is a greater risk.

And, as *Forbes* showed, the drug czar's office has grossly exaggerated the numbers on this issue in the past.

Meanwhile, UCLA public policy expert Mark Kleiman has pointed out that federally funded research by the University of Michigan shows that since the 1970s the level of high reported by high school seniors who smoked marijuana has remained "flat as a pancake." In other words, even if today's kids are smoking more potent stuff, they don't get higher than their folks did—like drinking a few whiskey shots rather than multiple mugs of beer, they use less of the good stuff to achieve the same effect.

Lies About Marijuana's Effect on Depression

With regard to depression, evidence of a causal role for marijuana is even murkier. In general, depression rates in the population did rise sharply during the time period in which marijuana use also skyrocketed. But there were so many other relevant sociological factors that marked the last half of the 20th century—rising divorce rates, the changing roles of women, economic shifts, and better diagnoses of psychiatric conditions, to name a few—that scientists have rarely focused on marijuana as a potential cause for the increase in depression. . . .

Moreover, a June 2005 study by researchers at University of Southern California, using the Center for Epidemiologic Studies' Depression Scale, found that marijuana use was in fact associated with lower levels of depression. Because the research was conducted using an Internet survey, it's possible that the most severely depressed people did not participate; nonetheless the study of more than 4,400 people found that both heavy pot smokers and moderate users reported less depression than did nonusers.

Dr. Myrna Weissman, a psychiatrist and leading epidemiologist of depression at Columbia University, sums up the current research and her view of marijuana's role in depression rates this way: "I can't imagine that it's a major factor." . . .

Losing Credibility

For a public desensitized to fear-mongering anti-drug messages, a campaign touting selected statistics from tenuous studies seems especially tone deaf, if not irresponsible.

"If I tell my 15-year-old that he's going to have a psychotic episode if he smokes pot, but he knows that his older brother already smokes pot and is fine, is he going to believe me when I tell him that methamphetamine damages the brain?" said Mitch Earleywine, an associate professor of psychology at the State University of New York at Albany, who coauthored the USC study. "What's going to happen is we're going to lose all credibility with our teens," Earleywine said.

The drug czar's office may soon face a full-blown credibility problem regarding its fight against marijuana.

Analyze the essay:

1. The author begins her essay by describing an antidrug advertisement that she thinks exaggerates the dangers of marijuana. Is this an effective way to start the essay? Explain your answer.
2. Authors Amodio and Szalavitz hold different views on whether marijuana is stronger today than it was in previous decades. Explain each author's position and side with the author you think better argued the point.

Marijuana Should Be Legal

Steve Maich

According to Steve Maich in the following essay, there are several benefits to legalizing marijuana. He argues that legalization would allow profits from marijuana sales to go toward government and social programs instead of to drug lords and gangs. When added to the money saved from fighting the war on drugs, Maich contends that the profits from a legalized and taxed marijuana industry could be enormous. Furthermore, he argues that marijuana is not harmful to health and is commonly used by all types of people. Continuing to prohibit the drug makes neither financial nor social sense, he concludes.

Maich is a writer for *Maclean's*, a weekly Canadian magazine from which this viewpoint was taken.

Consider the following questions:

1. According to the author, what was Canada's marijuana market worth in 2000?
2. How much does Canada spend annually fighting drug traffic, as reported by the author?
3. What was the finding of a 2002 report by the Senate Special Committee on Illegal Drugs on the harmfulness of marijuana?

W hen the day finally comes that this country legalizes the cultivation and sale of marijuana, compassion will not figure into the decision. Nor will weed be legitimized for the sake of any real or imagined medicinal benefits. And it won't be the various appeals to per-

Steve Maich, "A Case for Marijuana, Inc.," *Maclean's*, Vol. 117, November 22, 2004, p. 42.
© 2004 by *Maclean's Magazine*. Reproduced by permission.

sonal liberty that will swing the pendulum of our anti-quated drug laws. No, when Ottawa finally abandons the costly and futile effort to maintain pot prohibition, it will be the inescapable logic of the market that casts the deciding vote.

Missing Out on Substantial Profits

Hard as it may be to believe, Canada's biggest agricultural product is an illegal plant. Various estimates peg this country's cannabis trade at considerably more than $7 billion in annual sales—twice as much as pig farming brings in, and almost three times more than wheat does. Even the mighty cattle industry, at $5.2 billion a year in revenue, lags behind the marijuana business for sheer size. There is no formal market and cultivation has to be done surreptitiously, and still, nothing brings in the green like grass does.

So while timid federal politicians debate baby-step improvements to existing drug laws, a thriving industry carries on, completely indifferent to the government's dithering. The latest turn in the drug debate came this month when the Martin Liberals re-tabled legislation to decriminalize possession of small amounts of cannabis, while simultaneously proposing to increase maximum sentences for cultivation and trafficking. It's the same old drug war rolled in new papers. And even this may be too radical for parliamentarians.

Smoking Marijuana Is Commonplace

Thus far, no one has had the courage to stand up and call for real progress: legalization, regulation and taxation. As a result, the massive financial opportunity offered by making marijuana a commercial product remains out of reach. And while Ottawa fiddles, Canada smokes. Every day across this country people from all walks of life are getting high, getting hungry and falling asleep. If this sounds like a crisis to you, then you're qualified to be the Conservative justice critic.

A marijuana plant is displayed during an Ottawa rally on Parliament Hill. There is a growing movement to legalize marijuana in Canada.

Earlier this year, The Eraser Institute released a study of the British Columbia pot industry, estimating that the Canadian market alone was worth as much as $4.4 billion in 2000. That doesn't include exports. And the market is growing: according to the study, the number of Canadian pot smokers has risen by two-thirds in a decade. "To anyone with even a passing acquaintance with modern history, it is apparent that we are reliving the experience of alcohol prohibition of the early years of the last century," the report said.

The same conservative think tank that normally calls for privatized health care and tax cuts is now championing legalized pot, projecting that government could easily reap over $2 billion in annual revenue by taking control of the industry. This should be a sign to anyone in Ottawa with the guts to face it: when the neo-cons and hippies start agreeing on policy issues, it's a pretty good sign you've fallen behind a social trend.

Legalizing Marijuana Would Lower Crime and Violence

Just as importantly, the report points out, every dollar reaped by government regulation of the pot industry would be a dollar taken away from the criminal gangs that run the industry today. We'd save billions more by eliminating the staggering costs of a losing war. In 2001, Auditor General Sheila Fraser said the federal government was spending close to $500 million a year fighting the drug trade. Roughly 95 per cent of that goes to enforcement and policing, and two-thirds of the country's 50,000 annual drug arrests are for cannabis offences.

> ### A Right to Use Marijuana
>
> People have a right to use marijuana or any drug in any way they see fit—as medicine, as religious ritual, or simply to make themselves feel good, as long as they don't hurt anyone else in the process.
>
> Jeffrey A. Schaler, *Baltimore Sun*, May 12, 2003.

The big question, for most lawmakers, is how the United States would react to cannabis legalization in Canada. Opposition politicians are already fretting over potential trade retaliation, and U.S. Ambassador Paul Cellucci warned [in 2004] that border traffic might be slowed if our drug laws are significantly relaxed. That would be a shame, for both countries. Trade is a two-way street, and if the U.S. wants to hobble its own economy for the sake of keeping the scourge of marijuana at bay, then that's their right. But I suspect the bluster would pass soon enough. The amount of marijuana seized at the Mexican-U.S. border is more than TWO times greater than the amount caught heading south from Canada, and that hasn't dampened the Bush administration's eagerness for closer ties with Mexico.

Support for Reform of Marijuana Laws Is Growing

A CNN / Time Magazine poll found that Americans are increasingly tolerant of marijuana in society.

Do you favor or oppose the legalization of marijuana?

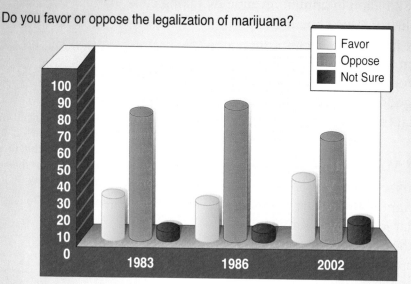

If marijuana is not legal, what should the penalty be for possession of small amounts of marijuana?

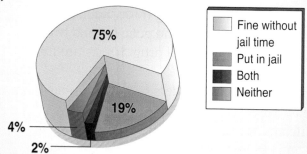

Do you think adults should be allowed to legally use marijuana for medical purposes?

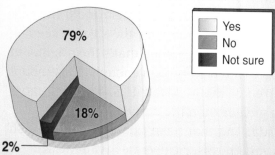

Source: CNN / Time Magazine poll, October 23-24, 2002.

Marijuana Is Safe Enough to Be Legal

As for the other familiar yarns about the dangers and evils of smoking a little weed, that it's addictive; that it is a "gateway" to hard-core drug use, etc.—it's worth reading the 2002 report of the Senate Special Committee on Illegal Drugs. It bluntly explodes many of those myths, propagated for decades by police forces and morality squads. After exhaustive study, it concludes that pot is a minimal health risk when used in moderation, and poses fewer social costs than other-legal-vices, like booze and cigarettes. In the words of the committee, "It is time to recognize what is patently obvious: our policies have been ineffective, because they are poor policies."

Two years have passed since the Senate recommended legalizing and regulating marijuana along lines similar to the tobacco industry. Perhaps one day the feds might find the courage to heed that advice and harness the power of supply and demand. In the meantime, all that potential tax revenue will keep rolling away while politicians and moralists keep blowing smoke.

Analyze the essay:

1. Instead of making an emotional or political argument, the author makes an economic argument for marijuana legislation. What do you think of this approach? What are its strengths? What are its weaknesses?

2. In describing those who oppose marijuana legalization, the author uses words such as "timid" and criticizes their lack of "courage" and "guts." How do these descriptions influence you while reading the essay? Do they help sway you, or do they turn you off to the author's point? Explain your reasoning.

Marijuana Should Be Illegal

John P. Walters

John P. Walters is the director of the White House Office of National Drug Control Policy (ONDCP), a federal agency that establishes policies and priorities for the national drug control program. In the following essay Walters claims that marijuana should remain prohibited because it is a dangerous drug that negatively affects society. Legalizing marijuana, he contends, would dramatically increase drug use among youth and result in hefty national health care and benefits costs. He debunks claims that laws against marijuana punish innocent offenders and also rejects arguments that marijuana should be legalized simply because many people have tried it. Walters concludes that marijuana is too dangerous to be legalized.

Consider the following questions:

1. Who does the author believe has been "mugged by reality"?
2. What types of health care and benefits costs does the author say will accompany marijuana legalization?
3. What percent of America's youth use marijuana on a monthly basis, according to Walters?

The prospect of a drug-control policy that includes regulated legalization has enticed intelligent commentators for years, no doubt because it offers, on the surface, a simple solution to a complex problem. Reasoned debate about the real consequences usually dampens

John P. Walters, "No Surrender: the Drug War Saves Lives," *National Review*, September 17, 2004, copyright© 2004 by National Review, Inc., 215 Lexington Avenue, New York, NY 10016. Reproduced by permission.

enthusiasm, leaving many erstwhile proponents feeling mugged by reality. . . .

Legalization Would Be Disastrous

The legalization scheme is . . . unworkable. A government-sanctioned program to produce, distribute, and tax an addictive intoxicant creates more problems than it solves.

First, drug use would increase. No student of supply-and-demand curves can doubt that marijuana would become cheaper, more readily available, and more widespread than it currently is when all legal risk is removed and demand is increased by marketing.

Second, legalization will not eliminate marijuana use among young people any more than legalizing alcohol eliminated underage drinking. If you think we can tax marijuana to where it costs more than the average teenager can afford, think again. Marijuana is a plant that can be readily grown by anyone. If law enforcement is unable to distinguish "legal" marijuana from illegal, growing marijuana at home becomes a low-cost (and low-risk) way to supply your neighborhood and friends. "Official marijuana" will not drive out the black market, nor will it eliminate the need for tough law enforcement. It will only make the task more difficult. . . .

Government-sanctioned marijuana would be a bonanza for trial lawyers (the government may wake up to find that it has a liability for the stoned trucker who plows into a school bus). Health-care and employment-benefits costs will increase (there is plenty of evidence that drug-using employees are less productive, and less healthy), while more marijuana use will further burden our education system.

> ## Protecting the Public Health
>
> Like speeding, drunken driving, smoking cigarettes in elevators and failing to buckle your seat belt in a car, possessing and selling marijuana are prohibited in order to protect the public health.
>
> Robert I. Dupont, *CQ Researcher*, February 11, 2005.

Marijuana Is Illegal Because It Is Dangerous

The truth is, there are laws against marijuana because marijuana is harmful. With every year that passes, medical research discovers greater dangers from smoking it, from links to serious mental illness to the risk of cancer, and even dangers from in utero exposure.

In fact, given the new levels of potency and the sheer prevalence of marijuana (the number of users contrasted with the number of those using cocaine or heroin), a case can be made that marijuana does the most social harm of any illegal drug. Marijuana

A drug dealer grows marijuana in his home. Experts believe the careful cultivation of the drug has increased its potency.

is currently the leading cause of treatment need: Nearly two-thirds of those who meet the psychiatric criteria for needing substance-abuse treatment do so because of marijuana use. For youth, the harmful effects of marijuana use now exceed those of all other drugs combined. Remarkably, over 40 percent of youths who are current marijuana smokers meet the criteria for abuse or dependency. In several states, marijuana smoking exceeds tobacco smoking among young people, while marijuana has become more important than alcohol as a factor in treatment for teenagers.

Prohibition Is Not the Problem

Legalizers assert that the justice system arrests 700,000 marijuana users a year, suggesting that an oppressive system is persecuting the innocent. This charge is a fraud. Less than 1 percent of those in prison for drug violations are low-level marijuana offenders, and many of these have "pled down" to the marijuana violation in the face of other crimes. The vast majority of those in prison on drug convictions are true criminals involved in drug trafficking, repeat offenses, or violent crime.

The value of legal control is that it enables judicial discretion over offenders, diverting minor offenders who need it into treatment while retaining the authority to guard against the violent and incorrigible. Further, where the sanction and supervision of a

GUESS WHAT TWO ISSUES THE LIBERALS ARE DEALING WITH FIRST...

KEEPING THIS POT SMOKER OUT OF JAIL...

MAKING SURE BOB AND PHIL CAN START PICKING OUT CHINA...

ENDING CHILD POVERTY.

Cardow. Reproduced by permission of Cagle Cartoons, Inc.

court are present, the likelihood of recovery is greatly increased. Removing legal sanction endangers the public and fails to help the offender.

Proponents of legalization argue that because approximately half of the referrals for treatment are from the criminal-justice system, it is the law and not marijuana that is the problem. Yet nearly half of all referrals for alcohol treatment likewise derive from judicial intervention, and nobody argues that drunk drivers do not really have a substance-abuse problem, or that it is the courts that are creating the perception of alcoholism. Marijuana's role in emergency-room cases has tripled in the past decade. Yet no judge is sending people to emergency rooms. They are there because of the dangers of the drug, which have greatly increased because of soaring potency.

Legalization Would Increase Drug Use

Legalization advocates suggest that youth will reduce their smoking because of this new potency. But when tobacco companies were accused of deliberately "spiking" their product with nicotine, no one saw this as a public-health gesture intended to reduce cigarette consumption. The deliberate effort to increase marijuana potency (and market it to younger initiates) should be seen for what it is—a steeply increased threat of addiction.

Proponents of legalization argue that the fact that 100 million Americans admit on surveys that they have tried marijuana in their lifetime demonstrates the public's acceptance of the drug. But the pertinent number tells a different story. There are approximately 15 million Americans, mostly young people, who report using marijuana on a monthly basis. That is, only about 6 percent of the population age twelve and over use marijuana on a regular basis.

To grasp the impact of legal control, contrast that figure with the number of current alcohol users (approximately 120 million). Regular alcohol use is eight times that of marijuana, and a large part of the difference is a

More Students Use Marijuana than Ever Before

	8th Grade		10th Grade		12th Grade	
	2004	2005	2004	2005	2004	2005
Past Month	6.4%	6.6%	15.9%	15.2%	19.9%	19.8%
Past Year	11.8	12.2	27.5	26.6	34.3	33.6
Lifetime	16.3	16.5	35.1	34.1	45.7	44.8

Source: National Institute on Drug Abuse and University of Michigan, Monitoring the Future 2005, December 2005.

function of laws against marijuana use. Under legalization, which would decrease the cost (now a little-noticed impediment to the young) and eliminate the legal risk, it is certain that the number of users would increase. Can anyone seriously argue that American democracy would be strengthened by more marijuana smoking?

Marijuana Should Be Illegal

The law itself is our safeguard, and it works. Far from being a hopeless battle, the drug-control tide is turning against marijuana. We have witnessed an 11 percent reduction in youth marijuana use over the last two years, while perceptions of risk have soared.

Make no mistake about what is going on here: Drug legalization is a worldwide movement, the goal of which is to make drug consumption—including heroin, cocaine, and methamphetamine—an acceptable practice. Using the discourse of rights without responsibilities, the effort strives to establish an entitlement to addictive substances. The impact will be devastating. Drug legalizers will not be satisfied with a limited distribution of medical marijuana, nor will they stop at legal marijuana for sale in convenience stores. Their goal is clearly identifiable: tolerated addiction.

Analyze the essay:

1. Does knowing the author is head of the White House Office of National Drug Control Policy influence your opinion of his argument? Explain why or why not.
2. Read the opening paragraphs of Walters's and Maich's essays. What strategy does each use to introduce his argument? Which do you believe is more effective? Explain.

Marijuana Has Medicinal Value

National Organization for the Reform of Marijuana Laws

The National Organization for the Reform of Marijuana Laws (NORML) has lobbied to end marijuana prohibition for over thirty years. In the following essay NORML maintains that marijuana has important medicinal value. The authors argue that even government-appointed commissions have concluded that marijuana has therapeutic potential. It provides relief from chronic pain, nausea, glaucoma, and the symptoms of movement disorders, and it stimulates the appetite for those suffering from HIV, NORML claims. For these reasons, the authors claim that qualifying patients under a doctor's supervision should have legal access to medicinal marijuana.

Consider the following questions:

1. When did Western doctors begin to recommend using marijuana to treat some disorders, as reported by the authors?
2. What government-appointed commissions have issued favorable findings on marijuana's medical potential?
3. What states have adopted medical marijuana laws according to the authors?

M arijuana prohibition applies to everyone, including the sick and dying. Of all the negative consequences of prohibition, none is as tragic as the denial of medicinal cannabis to the tens of thousands of patients who could benefit from its therapeutic use.

National Organization for the Reform of Marijuana Laws (NORML), Washington, DC: 2006. Reproduced by permission of the author.

Signe. Reproduce by permission of Cartoonists & Writers Syndicate/Cartoonweb.com.

The Evidence Supporting Marijuana's Medical Value

Written references to the use of marijuana as a medicine date back nearly 5,000 years. Western medicine embraced marijuana's medical properties in the mid-1800s, and by the beginning of the 20th century, physicians had published more than 100 papers in the Western medical literature recommending its use for a variety of disorders. Cannabis remained in the United States pharmacopoeia until 1941, removed only after Congress passed the Marihuana Tax Act which severely hampered physicians from prescribing it. The American Medical Association (AMA) was one of the most vocal organizations to testify against the ban, arguing that it would deprive patients of a past, present and future medicine.

Modern research suggests that cannabis is a valuable aid in the treatment of a wide range of clinical applications. These include pain relief—particularly of neuropathic pain (pain from nerve damage)—nausea, spasticity, glaucoma, and movement disorders. Marijuana is also a powerful appetite stimulant, specifically for patients suffering from HIV, the AIDS wasting syndrome, or dementia. Emerging research suggests that marijuana's medicinal properties may protect the body against some types of malignant tumors and are neuroprotective.

Health Organizations Support Medicinal Marijuana

Currently, more than 60 U.S. and international health organizations—including the American Public Health Association, Health Canada and the Federation of American Scientists—support granting patients immediate legal access to medicinal marijuana under a physician's supervision. Several others, including the American Cancer Society and the American Medical Association, support the facilitation of wide-scale, clinical research trials so that physicians may better assess cannabis' medical potential. In addition, a 1991 Harvard study found that 44 percent of oncologists had previously advised marijuana therapy to their patients. Fifty percent responded they would do so if marijuana was legal. A more recent national survey performed by researchers at Providence Rhode Island Hospital found that nearly half of physicians with opinions supported legalizing medical marijuana.

Government Commissions Back Legalization

Virtually every government-appointed commission to investigate marijuana's medical potential has issued favorable findings. These include the U.S. Institute of Medicine in 1982, the Australian National Task Force on Cannabis in 1994 and the U.S. National Institutes of Health Workshop on Medical Marijuana in 1997. . . .

Britain's House of Lord's Science and Technology Committee found in 1998 that the available evidence supported the legal use of medical cannabis. MPs determined: "The government should allow doctors to prescribe cannabis for medical use. . . . Cannabis can be effective in some patients to relieve symptoms of multiple sclerosis, and against certain forms of pain. . . . This evidence is enough to justify a change in the law." The Committee reaffirmed their support in a March 2001 follow-up report criticizing Parliament for failing to legalize the drug.

U.S. investigators reached a similar conclusion in 1999. After conducting a nearly two-year review of the medical literature, investigators at the National Academy of Sciences, Institute of Medicine affirmed: "Scientific data indicate the potential therapeutic value of cannabinoid drugs . . . for pain relief, control of nausea and vomiting, and appetite stimulation. . . . Except for the harms associated with smoking, the adverse effects of marijuana use are within the range tolerated for other medications." Nevertheless, the authors noted cannabis inhalation "would be advantageous" in the treatment of some diseases, and that marijuana's short-term medical benefits outweigh any smoking-related harms for some patients. Predictably, federal authorities failed to act upon the IOM's recommendations, and instead have elected to continue their long-standing policy of denying marijuana's medical value. . . .

Public Support for Medical Marijuana

Since 1996, voters in eight states—Alaska, Arizona, California, Colorado, Maine, Nevada, Oregon and Washington—have adopted initiatives exempting patients who use marijuana under a physician's supervision from state criminal penalties. [Since 2005 additional states have passed medical marijuana laws for a total of twelve.] In 1999, the Hawaii legislature ratified a similar law. These laws do not legalize marijuana or alter criminal penalties regarding the possession or cultivation of marijuana for recreational use. They merely provide a narrow exemption from state prosecution for defined patients who possess and use marijuana with their doctor's recommendation. Available evidence indicates that these laws are functioning as voters intended, and that reported abuses are minimal.

As the votes in these states suggest, the American public clearly distinguishes between the medical use and the recreational use of marijuana, and a majority support

Medical Marijuana Use in the U.S., 2005

States that permit marijuana use with a doctor's permission.

States that have research programs for medical marijuana.

States that have research programs for and permit use of medical marijuana.

Source: Issues & Controversies On File, Facts.com, July 8, 2005, www.2facts.com.

legalizing medical use for seriously ill patients. A March 2001 Pew Research Center poll reported that 73 percent of Americans support making marijuana legally available for doctors to prescribe, as did a 1999 Gallup poll. Similar support has been indicated in every other state and nationwide poll that has been conducted on the issue since 1995.

Analyze the essay:

1. NORML introduces the essay by appealing to a reader's concern for sick and dying people. Did you find this to be an effective strategy? Explain your reasoning.
2. In this essay NORML argues that marijuana has medicinal value. In the following essay Andrea Barthwell claims that marijuana is not medicine. What types of evidence does each author use to support his or her viewpoint? Which do you find more persuasive? Explain.

Marijuana Is Not Medicine

Andrea Barthwell

In the following essay Andrea Barthwell argues that no scientific evidence proves that marijuana is a safe and effective medicine. While some reports show that the compounds found in marijuana have potential medicinal value, Barthwell claims, they also state that smoking is not a safe way to administer medicine. The United States has established strict research and testing procedures that ensure the safety of medicines before they can be sold to the public. Marijuana, Barthwell argues, has failed to meet these tests. She therefore concludeds that marijuana should not be prescribed to patients.

Barthwell is a doctor and former deputy director of the White House Office of National Drug Control Policy.

Consider the following questions:

1. According to Barthwell, why did many Americans claim that they felt better when using patent "cures"?
2. What are researchers exploring to overcome the limitations of synthetic versions of marijuana, as reported by the author?
3. What dangerous substances does Barthwell report medical science has approved for medical use?

As a physician with more than 20 years of experience dealing with patients who are addicted to drugs, I am often asked my professional opinion about

Andrea Barthwell, "A Haze of Misinformation Clouds Issue of Medical Marijuana," *Los Angeles Times*, July 23, 2003. Reproduced by permission of the author.

a contentious public health question: What is the medical basis for smoking marijuana? The answer needs some context.

The Job of Modern Medicine

Americans today have the world's safest, most effective system of medical practice, built on a process of scientific research, testing and oversight that is unequaled.

Before the passage of the Pure Food and Drug Act in 1907, Americans were exposed to a host of patent medicine "cure-alls," everything from vegetable "folk remedies" to dangerous mixtures with morphine. The major component of most "cures" was alcohol, which probably explained why people reported that they "felt better."

Needless to say, claimed benefits were erratic and irreproducible.

Marijuana, whatever its value, is intoxicating, and it's not surprising that sincere people will report relief of their symptoms when they smoke it. The important point is that there is a difference between feeling better and actually getting better. It is the job of modern medicine to establish this distinction.

Setting the Record Straight

The debate over drug use generates a great deal of media attention—including the focus on the administration's appeal . . . to the U.S. Supreme Court against medical marijuana—and frequent misinformation. Some will have read, for instance, that the medicinal value of smoking marijuana represents "mainstream medical opinion." It is time to set the record straight.

After extensive testing, some scientists have concluded that marijuana has no medicinal value.

"SMOKE TWO JOINTS, AND CALL ME IN THE MORNING."

Schwadron. © Harley Schwadron. www.cartoonstock.com. Reproduced by permission.

Simply put, there is no scientific evidence that qualifies smoked marijuana to be called medicine. Further, there is no support in the medical literature that marijuana, or indeed any medicine, should be smoked as the preferred form of administration. The harms to health are simply too great.

Marijuana advocates often cite the 1999 National Academy of Science's Institute of Medicine report as justifying the drug's medical use. But, in fact, the verdict of that report was "marijuana is not a modern medicine." The institute was particularly troubled by the notion that crude marijuana might be smoked by patients, which it termed "a harmful drug-delivery system."

These concerns are echoed by the Food and Drug Administration, the agency charged with approving all medicines. As the FDA recently noted: "While there are no proven benefits to [smoked] marijuana use, there are many short- and long-term risks associated with marijuana use."

Exploring Better Delivery Systems

Compounds in the marijuana plant do potentially have a medical value. For instance, a synthetic version of an ingredient in marijuana has been approved for treating nausea for chemotherapy patients, as well as for treatment of anorexia associated with weight loss in patients with AIDS.

Admittedly, these medications have limitations, including the relatively slow onset of relief. Researchers are exploring drug-delivery systems that allow rapid relief—perhaps an oral inhalator like those used by asthma patients—as a response to patient needs.

But these medications are a far cry from burning the crude weed and gulping down the smoke. Every American is familiar with aspirin, and some know that it was first found in willow bark, from which the therapeutic agent acetylsalicylic acid was eventually synthesized. Surely no one today would chew willow bark, much less smoke a piece of tree, to cure a headache.

> ## No Place for Medical Marijuana
>
> There is no legitimate medical use whatsoever for marijuana. This is not medicine. This is bogus witchcraft. It has no place in medicine, no place in pain relief, and it has no place around our children.
>
> Former congressman Bob Barr (R-GA), debate with radio talk show host Neil Boortz, May 14, 2002.

A Need for Proof

Medical science does not fear any compound, even those with a potential for abuse. If a substance has the proven capacity to serve a medical purpose, then it will be accepted. We have done so with substances as dangerous as opium, allowing the medical use of many of its derivatives, including morphine, Demerol and OxyContin. The key term is "proven capacity." Only if compounds from marijuana pass the same tests of research scrutiny that any other drug must undergo will they become part of the modern medical arsenal.

Our investment in medical science is at risk if we do not defend the proven process by which medicines are brought to the market. All drugs must undergo rigorous clinical trials before a drug can be released for public use.

The overarching charge to any physician is: "First, do no harm." That is the test smoked marijuana cannot pass.

Analyze the essay:

1. Barthwell compares smoking marijuana to relieve pain to chewing willow bark to cure a headache. Do you think this is a logical comparison? Why or why not?
2. The goal of NORML, the author of the previous viewpoint, is to end marijuana prohibition. Andrea Barthwell, at the time her essay was written, was deputy director of the White House Office of National Drug Control Policy (ONDCP), which opposes the recreational and medical use of marijuana. Does knowing the background of the authors influence your opinion of their arguments in any way? Explain your opinion.

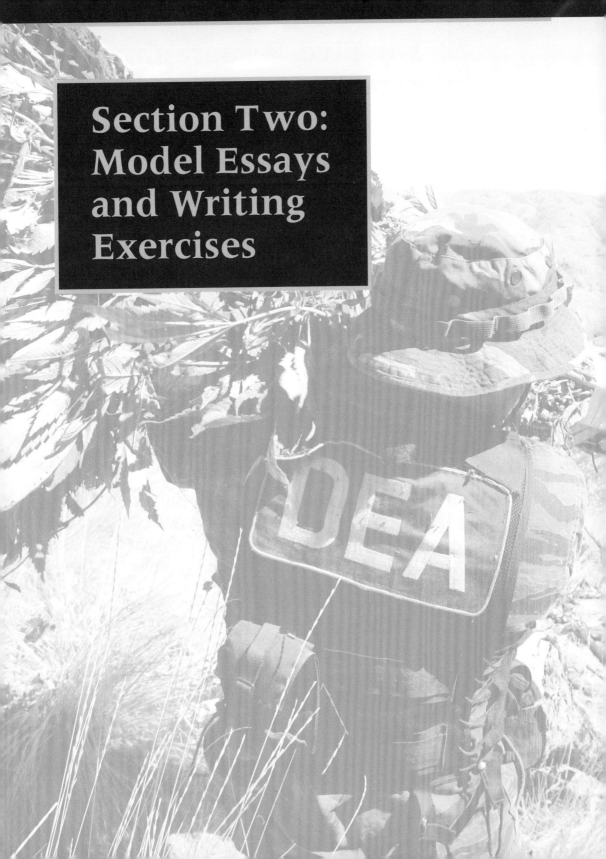

Section Two: Model Essays and Writing Exercises

The Five-Paragraph Essay

An *essay* is a short piece of writing that discusses or analyzes one topic. The five-paragraph essay is a form commonly used in school assignments and tests. Every five-paragraph essay begins with an *introduction*, ends with a *conclusion*, and features three *supporting paragraphs* in the middle.

The Thesis Statement. The introduction includes the essay's thesis statement. The thesis statement presents the argument or point the author is trying to make about the topic. The essays in this book all have different thesis statements because they are making different arguments about marijuana.

The thesis statement should clearly tell the reader what the essay will be about. A focused thesis statement helps determine what will be in the essay; the subsequent paragraphs are spent developing and supporting its argument.

The Introduction. In addition to presenting the thesis statement, a well-written introductory paragraph captures the attention of the reader and explains why the topic being explored is important. It may provide the reader with background information on the subject matter or feature an anecdote that illustrates a point relevant to the topic. It could also present startling information that clarifies the point of the essay or put forth a contradictory position that the essay will refute. Further techniques for writing an introduction are found later in this section.

The Supporting Paragraphs. The introduction is followed by three (or more) supporting paragraphs. These are the main body of the essay. Each paragraph presents and develops a *subtopic* that supports the essay's thesis statement. Each subtopic is then supported with its own facts, details, and examples. The writer can use various kinds of supporting material and details to back up the topic of each supporting paragraph. These may include statistics, quotations from people with special knowledge or expertise, historic facts, and anecdotes. A rule of writing is that specific and concrete examples are more convincing than vague, general, or unsupported assertions.

The Conclusion. The *conclusion* is the paragraph that closes the essay. Its function is to summarize or reiterate the main idea of the essay. It may recall an idea from the introduction or briefly examine the larger implications of the thesis. Because the conclusion is also the last chance a writer has to make an impression on the reader, it is important that it not simply repeat what has been presented elsewhere in the essay, but close it in a clear, final, and memorable way.

Although the order of the essay's component paragraphs is important, they do not have to be written in that order. Some writers like to decide on a thesis and write the introduction paragraph first. Other writers like to focus first on the body of the essay and write the introduction and conclusion later.

Pitfalls to Avoid

When writing essays about controversial issues such as marijuana, it is important to remember that disputes over the material are common precisely because there are many different perspectives. Remember to state your arguments in careful and measured terms. Evaluate your topic fairly—avoid overstating negative qualities of one perspective or understating positive qualities of another. Use examples, facts, and details to support any assertions you make.

The Expository Essay

The previous section of this book provided you with samples of published persuasive writing about marijuana. All were persuasive essays that made arguments or advocated a particular position about marijuana. But all included elements of *expository* writing as well.

Expository Essays vs. Persuasive Essays

Persuasive and expository essays have some similarities. Both can be about controversial topics. Both often involve research and the gathering of information, and may include citations or quotations from various sources.

Where they differ is not so much on *structure* as in *purpose*. The purpose of expository writing is to impart factual information about a particular subject matter to the reader. The writer seeks to demonstrate his/her knowledge of a topic by communicating that knowledge to the reader. In contrast, the purpose of a piece of persuasive writing is to argue in favor of a particular viewpoint or position and to convince readers that that particular view is correct. The writer's intent is to persuade the reader to agree with the essay or even to take a course of action.

In the real world, one often finds the two modes of writing intermixed. Sometimes the trickiest part of researching and writing about controversial topics is discerning where exposition ends and persuasion begins.

Types of Expository Writing

There are several different types of expository writing: definition, classification, process, illustration, and problem/solution. Examples of these types can be found in the viewpoints in the preceding section. The list below provides some ideas on how exposition could be organized and presented. Each type of writing could be used separately or in combination in five-paragraph essays.

Definition. Definition refers to simply explaining what something is. Definitions can be encompassed in a sentence. At other times, definitions may take a paragraph or more. The act of defining some topics—especially abstract concepts—can sometimes serve as the focus of entire essays. Of course people do not always agree on how some things should be defined, and in this way the definition expository essay can also be persuasive. In Viewpoint One, for example, Joseph V. Amodio defines marijuana as a dangerous drug. In Viewpoint Two, however, Maia Szalavitz defines marijuana as a harmless drug.

Classification. A classification essay describes and clarifies relationships between things by placing them in different categories, based on their similarities and differences. This can be a good way of organizing and presenting information. An essay with elements of classification is Viewpoint Three, by Steve Maich, in which he classifies the benefits of marijuana into various categories to reinforce his argument that marijuana should be legalized. He first describes the economic benefits legalization could bring farmers and to tax revenues. Next, Maich explains how legalizing marijuana could lower crime and violence. Finally, he argues that marijuana is safe enough to be legalized.

Process. A process essay looks at how something is done. The writer presents events or steps in a chronological or ordered sequence of steps. Process writing can either inform the reader of a past event or process by which something was made, or instruct the reader on how to do something.

Ilustration. Illustration is one of the simplest and most common patterns of expository writing. Simply put, it explains by giving specific and concrete examples. It is an effective technique for making one's writing both more interesting and more intelligible. In its essay NORML provides specific examples of organizations, commissions, and governments that support the medicinal use of marijuana such as the American Cancer Society, the Australian National Task Force on Cannabis, and states such as

Alaska, Maine, and Oregon. NORML also provides concrete examples of how marijuana is used as medicine. The organization claims that marijuana provides relief from the pain of nerve damage and stimulates appetite among patients with AIDS wasting syndrome.

Problem/Solution. In problem/solution essays the author raises a problem or a question, then uses the rest of the paragraph or essay to answer the question or provide possible resolutions to the problem. It can be an effective way to draw in the reader while imparting information to him/her.

Words and Phrases Common to Expository Essays

Writers use these words and phrases to explain their subjects, to provide transitions between paragraphs, and to summarize key ideas in an essay's concluding paragraph.

accordingly
because
clearly
consequently
first, . . . second, . . . third, . . .
for example
for this reason
from this perspective
furthermore
evidently
however

indeed
it is important to understand
it makes sense to
it seems as though
it then follows that
moreover
since
subsequently
therefore
this is why
thus

The Effects of Marijuana

Editor's Notes This first model essay is a "definition" expository essay that explains some of the effects of marijuana. Each paragraph contains supporting details and information, some of which was taken from resources found in Section One and Section Three of this book. The essay concludes with a paragraph that restates the essay's main idea—that marijuana is a controversial drug whose effects are disputed.

As you read this essay, pay attention to its components and how it is organized. Also note that all sources are cited using Modern Language Association (MLA) style. For more information on how to cite your sources, see Appendix C.* In addition, consider the following questions:

1. How does the introduction engage the reader's attention?
2. What kinds of supporting evidence are used to back up the essay's main points?
3. What purpose do the essay's quotes serve?

■ Refers to thesis and topic sentences

■ Refers to supporting details

Paragraph 1

Marijuana is the most commonly used illegal drug in the United States. According to the National Institute on Drug Abuse (NIDA), over 94 million Americans, 40 percent of the population, have tried marijuana. In addition to being the most commonly used illegal drug, marijuana is also the most controversial. While some commentators claim that marijuana is a dangerous drug that should remain illegal, others argue that marijuana is a relatively harmless drug that should be legal for recreational and medical use. In order to effectively evaluate the arguments made by people on both sides

This is the essay's thesis statement. It will determine what the essay will cover.

---

* In applying MLA style, the following simplifications have been made: Parenthetical text citations are confined to direct quotations only; electronic source documentation in the Works Cited list omits page ranges and some detailed facts of publication.

of the marijuana debate, it is important to understand marijuana's effects.

Paragraph 2

This is the topic sentence of the second paragraph.

The most immediate effect of marijuana is the feeling of intoxication, also known as the "high." These feelings begin as soon as the active ingredient in marijuana, delta-9-tetrahydrocannabinol (THC), enters the brain. THC stimulates brain cells to release the chemical dopamine, which is connected to feelings of pleasure. However, people who smoke marijuana have different reactions to the release of dopamine. For example, some people feel pleasant sensations. They see colors and hear sounds more intensely and suddenly become hungry or thirsty. Others, however, experience intense anxiety, paranoia, and panic.

Transitional phrases such as "however" and "for example" keep the ideas in the essay flowing.

Paragraph 3

This is the topic sentence of the third paragraph.

The effects of marijuana on the brain are more controversial. For example, opponents of marijuana claim marijuana causes long-term memory impairment and even brain damage. THC appears to alter the way information is processed by the hippocampus, the part of the brain that controls the formation of memories. NIDA contends that "heavy marijuana use impairs a person's ability to form memories, recall events, and shift attention from one thing to another," NIDA and others cite such information when arguing against legalizing marijuana. Those who support legalization, however, maintain that marijuana does not permanently impair memory. According to Jared M. Fleisher and Tobias G. Snyder of the Harvard Coalition for Drug Policy Reform, "The ability to learn and recall new information is impaired while high, but the effects are neither long term nor irreversible." To support their claim, Fleisher and Snyder cite a study on marijuana and memory from Johns Hopkins University. Initially, marijuana users did poorly on tests compared to nonusers. However, after twenty-seven days, there were no differences in test performance between marijuana users and nonusers.

Quote from reputable sources to be sure you use quality information in your essay.

"Allegations that marijuana smoking alters brain function or has long-term effects on cognition," writes Paul Armentano of the National Organization for the Reform of Marijuana Laws, "are reckless and scientifically unfounded."

Paragraph 4

Another controversial effect of marijuana is its impact on the respiratory system. Some analysts claim that the risk of developing lung cancer from smoking marijuana is greater than from smoking cigarettes. For example, NIDA argues that because marijuana users tend to inhale more deeply and hold their breath longer than those who smoke cigarettes, marijuana smokers increase their lungs' exposure to cancer-causing smoke. "Puff for puff," NIDA claims, "smoking marijuana may increase the risk of cancer more than smoking tobacco does." (National 5). Fleisher and Snyder dispute these claims. They contend that cigarettes are more harmful than marijuana because cigarette smokers inhale more smoke over time than marijuana smokers do, and cigarette smoke damages smaller lung airways. Moreover, they claim, "while there has not been a single death reported from cannabis, cigarettes kill 430,000 people annually."

What is the topic sentence of paragraph 4?

Use quotes to express impassioned or particularly lively ideas.

Paragraph 5

The dispute over the relative dangers of cigarette and marijuana smoke is a prime example of the tension between those who believe marijuana is a dangerous drug and those who believe it is relatively harmless. Because the federal government currently views the effects of marijuana as a serious threat to pubic health, it has been classified as a dangerous drug with no medicinal value. Thus using, possessing, or selling marijuana is a serious crime with severe punishment. However, many analysts argue that the criminalization of marijuana is too costly. In their opinion marijuana is a significantly less dangerous drug than alcohol and tobacco, which are legal.

This is the essay's conclusion.

Since analysts on both sides of the marijuana debate have come to different conclusions about the effects of marijuana, the controversy over marijuana legalization will continue to remain heated.

Works Cited

Armentano, Paul. *The 2005 NORML Truth Report.* NORML 21 July 2005 accessed 9 Oct. 2006 < http://www.norml.org/index.cfm?Group_ID = 5513 > .

Fleisher, Jared M., and Tobias G. Snyder. "Marijuana Reconsidered." *Harvard Crimson* 7 Mar. 2002 accessed 11 Oct. 2006 < http://www.thecrimson.com/article.aspx?ref = 180429 > .

National Institute on Drug Abuse (NIDA). "Marijuana." *Research Report Series* (Bethesda, MD: NIH, July 2005).

Exercise A: Create an Outline from an Existing Essay

It often helps to create an outline of the five-paragraph essay before you write it. The outline can help you organize the information, arguments, quotes, and evidence you have gathered with your research.

For this exercise, create an outline that could have been used to write *Essay One: The Effects of Marijuana*. This "reverse engineering" exercise is meant to help familiarize you with how outlines can help classify and arrange information.

To do this you will need to
  1. articulate the essay's thesis,
  2. pinpoint important pieces of evidence,
  3. flag quotes that support the essay's ideas, and
  4. identify key points that support the argument.

Part of the outline has already been started to give you an idea of the assignment.

Outline
Write the essay's thesis:

I. Paragraph 2 topic: One effect of marijuana is intoxication.

  A.

  B. For some, marijuana intoxication is a pleasant experience.

  C.

II. Paragraph 3 topic:

A. Those who oppose marijuana legalization claim marijuana impairs memory.

    1.

    2. NIDA quote: "heavy marijuana use impairs a person's ability to form memories, recall events, and shift attention from one thing to another."

B.

    1.

    2.

III. Paragraph 4 topic:

A.

    1. Marijuana smokers inhale more deeply and hold their breath longer.
    2.

B. Cigarettes are more harmful than marijuana.

    1.

    2. Fleisher and Snyder quote: "while there has not been a single death reported from cannabis, cigarettes kill 430,000 people annually."

Marijuana Should Be Legal

Editor's Notes One way of writing an expository essay is to use the problem/solution method. A problem/solution essay raises a problem and then uses the rest of the essay to answer or provide possible solutions to the problem. The following sample essay uses problem/solution to show how legalizing marijuana could solve the problems that have been created by marijuana prohibition. The author first describes some of the societal costs of marijuana prohibition. The essay's supporting paragraphs then explain how legalization would put an end to these problems.

This essay differs from the previous essay in that it is persuasive, meaning that it attempts to convince the reader of a particular point of view. Pay attention to the ways in which certain phrases attempt to persuade you of the author's viewpoint.

As you read, answer the questions raised by the notes in the margins. They will help you analyze how the essay is organized and how it is written.

■ Refers to thesis and topic sentences

■ Refers to supporting details

Paragraph 1

Since 1990 over 7.2 million Americans—more than the combined populations of Alaska, Delaware, the District of Columbia, Hawaii, Montana, North Dakota, South Dakota, Rhode Island, Vermont, and Wyoming—have been arrested on marijuana charges. Although marijuana use has not increased since 1990, the number of marijuana arrests has more than doubled. Even more disturbing is that 90 percent of these arrests were for mere possession, not for the more serious crime of trafficking and selling marijuana. This war on marijuana is too costly for the American people. Millions of Americans are needlessly persecuted for the use of a relatively harmless drug, and American taxpayers are paying the price. To end the needless persecution of American citizens and the waste of

How does the author capture the interest of the reader in the introduction?

What is the essay's thesis statement?

resources on a war that has failed to deter marijuana use, the government should legalize marijuana.

Paragraph 2

What is the topic sentence of Paragraph 2?

One of the primary reasons that marijuana should be legalized is that it is a harmless drug. In fact, marijuana is probably the least dangerous of the mind-altering drugs, including those that are legal, such as alcohol. According to the Centers for Disease Control (CDC), there are approximately 46,000 non-vehicle-related, alcohol-induced deaths each year. More than 440,000 people die each year from smoking tobacco. However, no one has ever died of an overdose of marijuana. Numerous studies and reports claim that marijuana is a relatively safe drug compared to others. The editors of the *Lancet*, Britain's premier medical journal, assert that "the smoking of cannabis, even long-term, is not harmful to health" ("Deglamorising" 1241). Indeed, the penalties imposed by marijuana prohibition cause greater harm than the drug itself. Paul Armentano, a policy analyst for the National Organization for the Reform of Marijuana Laws (NORML), concludes, "By far the greatest danger to health posed by the use of marijuana stems from a criminal arrest and/or conviction" (2005). The severe criminal penalties for marijuana use outweigh the danger. To remedy this inequity, the harsh penalties that currently exist for marijuana use should be abolished. We must recognize that marijuana is not causing anyone great harm.

What authorities are quoted throughout the essay?

Paragraph 3

What is the topic sentence of Paragraph 3?

In addition to removing unnecessarily harsh penalties for a relatively harmless drug, a second reason the government should legalize marijuana is to end the needless waste of American tax dollars. Economics professor Jeffrey A. Miron and marijuana reform activist Jon Gettman report that each year state and local taxpayers spend between $5.3 billion and $7.7 billion and the federal government spends $4 billion arresting and prosecuting individuals for marijuana violations. This money is spent on housing, health care, attorney fees, court coats, and other expenses needed to arrest, prosecute, and incarcerate otherwise peaceful American citizens who enjoy smoking marijuana the same way some enjoy having an alcoholic beverage. These funds would be better spent chasing real criminals such as murderers and terrorists. "Federal efforts would undoubtedly be better served keeping a bomb out of the hands of Al Qaeda [terrorists]," writes the California chapter of NORML, "than keeping a bong out of the hands of a marijuana smoker" (Krane).

Paragraph 4

Not only does prohibition waste resources, it has also failed to deter the use of marijuana, a final reason to legalize its recreational use. "Marijuana enforcement," says Armentano, "has had no discernable long-term impact on marijuana availability or use" (2005). Indeed, more Americans than ever have tried marijuana. The U.S. Department of Health and Human Services *2003 National Household Survey on Drug Abuse* revealed that some 2.6 million Americans tried marijuana for the first time in 2003, a higher rate than the 1.5 million reported in 1990 and the 0.8 million in 1965. Clearly, prohibition has had no deterrent effect on the American public. Instead, it has created many problems. "Prohibition and the resulting black market enriches criminals and terrorists, results in gang warfare, encourages the recruitment of youth to sell drugs, [and] provides youth with easier access to drugs," claims Scott Ehlers of the Drug Policy Foundation. It is clear that prohibiting marijuana does more harm than good.

What is the topic sentence of Paragraph 4?

What transitional phrases are used to keep the essay moving?

Paragraph 5

Prohibiting marijuana creates crime, costs billions, and ruins lives while doing nothing to stem its use. The best way to end the economic and social ills created by prohibition is to legalize the recreational use of marijuana by adults. Approximately 80 million Americans admit to

What is the essay's conclusion?

having at one time used marijuana, including former president Bill Clinton and former House speaker Newt Gingrich. "Nearly 15 million Americans admit to being current users of cannabis," writes Armentano. "It is time for America's marijuana laws to reflect this reality, not deny it" (2005).

Works Cited

"Deglamorising Cannabis." *Lancet* 11 Nov. 1995.

Armentano, Paul. *The 2005 NORML Truth Report,* NORML 21 July 2005, accessed 11 Oct. 2006 < www.norml.org/index. cfm?Group_ID = 5513 > .

---. "Should Marijuana Laws Be Relaxed? Yes." *CQ Researchers* 11 Feb. 2005: 125–48.

Ehlers, Scott. Testimony before Subcommittee on Criminal Justice, Drug Policy, and Human Resources hearing on "Drug Legalization, Criminalization, and Harm Reduction." 16 June 1999.

Krane, Kris. "Crackdown on Marijuana Pipes a Senseless Waste of Law Enforcement Resources—More Prosecutions for Bongs than Terror." Accessed 11 Oct. 2006 Cal NORML < www.canorml.org/news/pipedreams.html > .

Exercise A: Create an Outline from an Existing Essay

As you did for the first model essay in this section, create an outline that could have been used to write "Marijuana Should Be Legal." Be sure to identify the essay's thesis statement, its supporting ideas, and key pieces of evidence that are used.

Exercise B: Create an Outline for an Opposing Expository Essay

For this exercise, your assignment is to find supporting ideas, create an outline, and ultimately write an expository essay that argues a view that opposes that of the second model essay. Using information from Section One and Section Three of this book and your own research, you will write an essay that supports the following thesis statement: Marijuana should remain illegal.

Part I. Brainstorm and collect information.

Before you begin writing, you will need to think carefully about what ideas your essay will contain. Coming up with these ideas is a process known as *brainstorming*. Brainstorming involves jotting down any ideas that might make good material when you finally begin to write.

Begin the brainstorming process by simply asking yourself, in what ways would the recreational use of marijuana pose a threat? Use outside research or the material in Section One and Section Three in this book to come up with at least three arguments. Each one should illustrate a clear reason why the recreational use of marijuana should remain illegal.

For each of the ideas you come up with, write down facts or information that support it. These could be

- statistical information,
- direct quotations,
- anecdotes of past events.

Example Paragraph Topic Sentence: One reason why marijuana must remain illegal is because it is a dangerous drug.

- Joseph V. Amodio's claims that marijuana reduces motivation and interest in friends and school and is a gateway to harder drugs.
- The study mentioned in Viewpoint One that showed marijuana has a long-lasting impact on the reaction time of airline pilots.
- John P. Walters quote from Viewpoint Four: "There are laws against marijuana because marijuana is harmful. With every year that passes, medical research discovers greater dangers from smoking it, from links to serious mental illness to the risk of cancer."

Sometimes you can develop ideas by critically examining the claims your opponent makes. For example, the model essay argues that prohibition has not deterred marijuana use among citizens; to the contrary, marijuana is popular and commonplace. For this reason, it should be made legal. Yet is this reasonable? Remember Viewpoint Four in Section One. In his essay John P. Walters challenges the idea that marijuana use has become acceptable or commonplace. According to him, just 6 percent of the population twelve and over use marijuana on a regular basis—hardly the majority of people. Learn to look for information like this that could potentially be used to challenge a particular claim.

Come up with two other points that support your thesis statement.

Part II. Place the information from Part I in outline form.

Part III. Write the arguments in paragraph form.

You now have three arguments that support the paragraph's thesis statement, as well as supporting material.

Use the outline to write out your three supporting arguments in paragraph form. Make sure each paragraph has a topic sentence that states the paragraph's thesis clearly and broadly. Then, add supporting sentences that express the facts, quotes, and examples that support the paragraph's argument. The paragraph may also have a concluding or summary sentence.

The Medical-Marijuana Debate

Editor's Notes The expository essay is a good medium for explaining complicated subjects to an audience. The following essay demonstrates such a style by exploring the medical-marijuana debate. However, unlike the second of the previous model essays, this essay does not attempt to make a persuasive argument. It concerns itself with laying out information for the reader in a clear and illustrative way.

This essay also differs from the previous model essays in that it is longer than five paragraphs. Many ideas require more paragraphs for adequate development. Moreover, the ability to write a sustained research or position paper is a valuable skill. Learning how to develop a longer piece of writing gives you the tools you will need to advance academically.

As you read, consider the questions posed in the margins. Continue to identify thesis statements, topic sentences, supporting details, transitions, and quotations. Examine the introductory and concluding paragraphs to understand how they give shape to the essay. Finally, evaluate the essay's general structure and assess its overall effectiveness.

Refers to thesis and topic sentences

Refers to supporting details

Paragraph 1

Meet Angel McClary Raich of Oakland, California. Since 1995 she has suffered from an inoperable brain tumor and other untreatable conditions that at one point left her confined to a wheelchair and in constant pain. In 1997 a nurse who knew of her suffering asked if Raich might consider using medical marijuana to ease her pain. At first Raich was offended by the suggestion. "I was very conservative. I was taught that drugs are bad. And I followed the law. I've never even gotten a speeding ticket," she said. (qtd. in Nieves A3) However, after conventional medicines

Why do you think the author chose to open her essay with this anecdote?

74

failed to alleviate her suffering and improve her quality of life, she began to seriously consider marijuana. Since her state had approved the use of medical marijuana in 1996, Raich decided to try it. She joined the Oakland Cannabis Buyers Cooperative, an organization that provides medical-grade marijuana cultivated specifically for patients such as Raich. Her pain eased, her appetite increased, and she was eventually strong enough to leave her wheelchair and walk again.

Paragraph 2

Raich is one of many Americans who are at the center of a vigorous controversy: the debate over whether marijuana has medical properties and whether it should be legalized as a medicine. Some groups consider marijuana to be a medicine that can treat a variety of medical conditions. According to the Marijuana Policy Project (MPP), an organization that supports marijuana's use as medicine, the drug reduces the nausea, vomiting, and loss of appetite that accompanies the side effects of chemotherapy, a treatment for cancer. The federal government, however, considers marijuana to be an extremely dangerous, highly addictive drug with no medicinal value. Thus, while voters in several states have approved the use of medical marijuana, it remains an illegal substance: Those who cultivate, sell, or use marijuana are subject to federal prosecution. This unresolved tension makes medical marijuana a hotly contested issue. In order to fully understand the medical-marijuana debate, it is important to examine the history of marijuana law and the arguments for and against its use as medicine.

What is the essay's thesis statement?

Paragraph 3

Marijuana was first used as a medicine thousands of years ago. In 2737 B.C. Chinese emperor Shen Neng used marijuana to treat gout, malaria, and rheumatism, among other diseases. Marijuana spread through Asia and Europe and ultimately reached the United States in the

Where is this paragraph's topic sentence?

mid-1800s. The drug was not initially considered to be dangerous. In fact, in the early 1900s several respectable American pharmaceutical companies such as Eli Lilly and Parke-Davis used marijuana extracts in their medicines. But over time, concern grew over whether marijuana was in fact a dangerous drug. In 1937 Congress passed the Marijuana Tax Act of 1937. Although the act did not prohibit marijuana, it required users to pay a tax on the drug. This reduced its popularity, and after 1942 the drug was rarely prescribed. Decades later Congress passed the Controlled Substances Act in 1970, which placed illegal and prescription drugs into five "schedules" or categories. Marijuana was placed in Schedule I, and thus categorized as a dangerous drug with no legitimate medicinal use. This classification effectively made marijuana illegal under federal law.

Note how this paragraph puts marijuana prohibition into historical context so the reader has background information on the topic.

Paragraph 4

Despite federal laws prohibiting marijuana, recreational use of the drug continued, and interest was rekindled in the drug's potential medicinal benefits. By 2006, voters in twelve states had passed initiatives that legalized marijuana's use for medicinal purposes. But the federal government disapproved of these initiatives on the grounds that marijuana is illegal and dangerous. In protest, the federal government sent armed squads of federal agents into California, one of the states that legalized medical marijuana, to break up its medical marijuana cooperatives. This meant that people such as Angel Raich could not get access to their medicine and accused the government of interfering with their ability to manage their health. It is at this crossroads where opponents and supporters of medical marijuana remain stuck.

What transitions are used to keep the essay moving?

Paragraph 5

Those who oppose medical marijuana argue that the medical-marijuana movement is simply part of an overall movement to legalize all drugs. The organizations that support medical marijuana, they claim, take advantage of people's compassion for the seriously ill to promote their ultimate goal—the legalization of the recreational use of all drugs. According to the Drug Enforcement Agency, the federal agency responsible for enforcing America's drug laws, "The campaign to allow marijuana to be used as medicine is a tactical maneuver in an overall strategy to completely legalize all drugs. Pro-legalization groups have transformed the debate from decriminalizing drug use to one of compassion and care for people with serious diseases" ("Exposing").

Note how this essay does not argue a point or attempt to persuade the reader, but neutrally illustrates its subjects in an attempt to explain the topic.

Paragraph 6

Medical-marijuana opponents also argue that marijuana has no proven benefits as medicine. "Marijuana is not medicine. It is an impure, smoked, herbal substance that has substantial side effects and substantial potential for abuse," writes Eric Voth, chairman of the Institute on Global Drug Policy (qtd. in "Update"). Indeed, the Food and Drug Administration, the agency in charge of approving medicines for use, does not consider marijuana to be anything but a dangerous drug. Furthermore, it is possible that marijuana could pose a danger to the severely ill if they are misled to believe that marijuana is a safe medicine. Calvina Fay, executive director of Drug Free America Foundation, warns, "We don't want truly sick and dying people to be scammed into thinking they are being medically treated by smoking pot. We believe that people who are truly sick need good, legitimate medicine" (Patients," 2005).

What authorities have been quoted in the essay? What are their qualifications for speaking on the subject?

Paragraph 7

But those who support the legal use of medical marijuana believe it has legitimate medicinal benefits. They contend that medical marijuana can help the seriously ill by alleviating pain, reducing nausea, and stimulating the appetite when other medications fail. In fact, according to the Marijuana Policy Project, marijuana can reduce the muscle pain and spasms of multiple sclerosis, the eye damage of glaucoma, and in some patients marijuana can prevent epileptic seizures. If this is true, then the federal government's restriction of medical marijuana could hurt patients' ability to manage their pain. "The fact of the matter is, the federal government is playing politics with patients' lives," argues Robert Raich, Angel Raich's husband. He accuses the government of "choosing to ignore the scientific and medical facts that cannabis is a good medicine for many patients" (qtd. in "Patients, States").

Paragraph 8

Those who support the medical use of marijuana also argue that federal interference with state medical marijuana laws violates states' rights, the right of each state to enact its own health policies. After all, the federal government has limited powers that are listed in the U.S. Constitution, and DEA raids on state-approved medical marijuana cooperatives are not included in those powers. This is interpreted by some as an abuse of federal power. For example, U.S. Supreme Court justice Sandra Day O'Connor reminds us that the American system is set up to allow states to experiment with policies that their citizens approve. As O'Connor has written, "One of federalism's chief virtues . . . is that it promotes innovation by allowing for the possibility that "a single courageous state may, if its citizens choose, serve as a laboratory; and try novel social and economic experiences without risk to the rest of the country," (qtd. in National). Prohibiting medical marijuana even after state voters approve it seems to violate this arrangement.

Note how the conclusion returns to a discussion of the problems faced by Raich, a subject introduced at the start of the essay.

Paragraph 9

For all of these reasons, the debate over medical marijuana rages on. While popular support for medical marijuana continues, so does the federal government's vigorous campaign against it. Because this complicated issue is not likely to be resolved any time soon, terminal patients such as Angel Raich may not have time to see the outcome.

Works Cited

"Exposing the Myth of Medical Marijuana." U.S. Drug Enforcement Agency. Accessed 11 Oct. 2006. < www.us doj.gov/dea/ongoing/marijuanaap.html > .

"Patients, States Adjust to New Marijuana Ruling." NPR Talk of the Nation 7 Jun 2005, accessed 11 Oct 2006 < http://www.npr.org/templates/story/story.php?story_ ID=4684123 > .

"Update: Medical Marijuana." *Issues & Controversies on File* 8 July 2005 < www.2facts.com > .

Barthwell, Andrea. "A Haze of Misinformation Clouds Issue of Medical Marijuana." *Los Angeles Times* 22 July 2003.

National Organization for the Reform of Marijuana Laws. "Medical Use: Introduction." NORML 12 July 2003 < www.norml.org/index.cfm?Group_ID = 5441 > .

Nieves, Evelyn. "'I Really Consider Cannabis My Miracle': Patients Fight to Keep Drug of Last Resort." *Washington Post* 1 Jan. 2005.

Exercise A: Examining Introductions and Conclusions

Every essay features introductory and concluding paragraphs that are used to frame the main ideas being presented. Along with presenting the essay's thesis statement, well-written introductions should grab the attention of the reader and make clear why the topic being explored is important. The conclusion reiterates the essay's thesis and is also the last chance for the writer to make an impression on the reader. Strong introductions and conclusions can greatly enhance an essay's effect on an audience.

The Introduction

There are several techniques that can be used to craft an introductory paragraph. An essay can start with

- an anecdote: a brief story that illustrates a point relevant to the topic;
- startling information: facts or statistics that elucidate the point of the essay;
- setting up and knocking down a position: a position or claim believed by proponents of one side of a controversy, followed by statements that challenge that claim;
- historical perspective: an example of the way things used to be that leads into a discussion of how or why things work differently now;
- summary information: general introductory information about the topic that feeds into the essay's thesis statement.

Problem One

Reread the introductory paragraphs of the model essays and of the viewpoints in Section One. Identify which of the techniques described above are used in the example essays. How do they grab the attention of the reader? Are their thesis statements clearly presented?

Problem Two

Write an introduction for the essay you have outlined and partially written in the previous exercise using one of the techniques described above.

The Conclusion

The conclusion brings the essay to a close by summarizing or returning to its main ideas. Good conclusions, however, go beyond simply repeating these ideas. Strong conclusions explore a topic's broader implications and reiterate why it is important to consider. They may frame the essay by returning to an anecdote featured in the opening paragraph. Or they may close with a quotation or refer back to an event in the essay. In opinionated essays, the conclusion can reiterate which side the essay is taking or ask the reader to reconsider a previously held position on the subject.

Problem Three

Reread the concluding paragraphs of the model essays and of the viewpoints in Section One. Which were most effective in driving their arguments home to the reader? What sorts of techniques did they use to do this? Did they appeal emotionally to the reader, or bookend an idea or event referenced elsewhere in the essay?

Problem Four

Write a conclusion for the essay you have outlined and partially written in the previous exercise using one of the techniques described above.

Author's Checklist

✔ Review the five-paragraph essay you wrote.

✔ Make sure it has a clear introduction that draws the reader in and contains a thesis statement that concisely expresses what your essay is about.

✔ Evaluate the paragraphs and make sure they each have clear topic sentences that are well supported by interesting and relevant details.

✔ Check that you have used compelling and authoritative quotes to enliven the essay.

✔ Finally, be sure you have a solid conclusion that uses one of the techniques presented in this exercise.

Exercise B: Using Quotations to Enliven Your Essay

No essay is complete without quotations. Get in the habit of using quotes to support at least some of the ideas in your essays. Quotes do not need to appear in every paragraph, but often enough so that the essay contains voices aside from your own. When you write, use quotations to accomplish the following:

- Provide expert advice that you are not necessarily in the position to know about
- Cite lively or passionate passages
- Include a particularly well-written point that gets to the heart of the matter
- Supply statistics or facts that have been derived from someone's research
- Deliver anecdotes that illustrate the point you are trying to make
- Express first-person testimony

There are a few important things to remember when using quotations:

- Note your sources' qualifications and biases. This way your reader can identify the person you have quoted and can put their words in a context.
- Put any quoted material within proper quotation marks. Failing to attribute quotes to their authors constitutes plagiarism, which is when an author takes someone else's words or ideas and presents them as his or her own. Plagiarism is a very serious infraction and must be avoided at all costs.

Problem One: Reread the essays presented in all sections of this book and find at least one example of each of the above quotation types.

Write Your Own Expository Five-Paragraph Essay

Using the information from this book, write your own five-paragraph expository essay that deals with marijuana. The following steps are suggestions on how to get started.

Step One: Choose your topic.
Think carefully before deciding on the topic of your expository essay about marijuana. Is there any subject that particularly fascinates you? Is there an issue you strongly support, or feel strongly against? Is there a topic you would like to learn more about? Ask yourself such questions before selecting your essay topic. Refer to Appendix D: Sample Essay Topics if you need help selecting a topic.

Step Two: Write down questions and answers about the topic.
Before you begin writing, you will need to think carefully about what ideas your essay will contain. This is a process known as *brainstorming*. Brainstorming involves asking yourself questions and coming up with ideas to discuss in your essay. Possible questions that will help you with the brainstorming process include:

- Why is this topic important?
- Why should people be interested in this topic?
- How can I make this essay interesting to the reader?
- What question am I going to address in this paragraph or essay?
- What facts, ideas, or quotes can I use to support the answer to my question?
- Will the question's answer reveal a preference for one subject over another?

Questions especially for expository essays include:

- Do I want to write an informative essay or an opinionated essay?
- Will I need to explain a process or course of action?
- Will my essay contain many definitions or explanations?
- Is there a particular problem that needs to be solved?

Step Three: Gather facts and ideas related to your topic.
This book contains several places to find information, including the viewpoints and the appendixes. In addition, you may want to research the books, articles, and Web sites listed in Section Three, or do additional research in your local library.

Step Four: Develop a workable thesis statement.
Use what you have written down in steps two and three to help you articulate the main point or argument you want to make in your essay. It should be expressed in a clear sentence and make an arguable or supportable point.

Examples:

Marijuana has been inaccurately classified as a dangerous drug with no medicinal value.

> This could be the thesis statement of an opinionated expository essay that defines and illustrates the different drug classifications in order to argue that marijuana has been incorrectly classified as a Schedule I drug.

Many people and organizations have shaped public attitudes toward marijuana use and marijuana prohibition.

> This could be the thesis statement of an informative expository essay that illustrates the history of the marijuana controversy by introducing the specific people and organizations who have led the debate.

Step Five: Write an outline or diagram.
1. Write the thesis statement at the top of the outline.
2. Write roman numerals I, II, and III on the left side of the page with A, B, and C under each numeral.
3. Next to each roman numeral, write down the best ideas you came up with in step three. These should all directly relate to and support the thesis statement.
4. Next to each letter write down information that supports that particular idea.

Step Six: Write the three supporting paragraphs.
Use your outline to write the three supporting paragraphs. Write down the main idea of each paragraph in sentence form. Do the same thing for the supporting points of information. Each sentence should support the paragraph of the topic. Be sure you have relevant and interesting details, facts, and quotes. Use transitions when you move from idea to idea to keep the text fluid. Sometimes, although not always, paragraphs can include a concluding or summary sentence that restates the paragraph's argument.

Step Seven: Write the introduction and conclusion.
See Essay Three Exercise A for information on writing introductions and conclusions.

Step Eight: Read and rewrite.
As you read, check your essay for the following:

✔ Does the essay maintain a consistent tone?

✔ Do all sentences serve to reinforce your general thesis or your paragraph theses?

✔ Do all paragraphs flow from one to the other? Do you need to add transition words or phrases?

✔ Have you quoted from reliable, authoritative, and interesting sources?

✔ Is there a sense of progression throughout the essay?

✔ Does the essay get bogged down in too much detail or irrelevant material?

✔ Does your introduction grab the reader's attention?

✔ Does your conclusion reflect back on any previously discussed material, or give the essay a sense of closure?

✔ Are there any spelling or grammatical errors?

Tips on Writing Effective Expository Essays

- You do not need to include every detail on your subjects. Focus on the most important ones that support your thesis statement.
- Vary your sentence structure; avoid repeating yourself.
- Maintain a professional, objective tone of voice. Avoid sounding uncertain or insulting.
- Anticipate what the reader's counterarguments may be and answer them.
- Use sources that state facts and evidence.
- Avoid assumptions or generalizations without evidence.
- Aim for clear, fluid, well-written sentences that together make up an essay that is informative, interesting, and memorable.

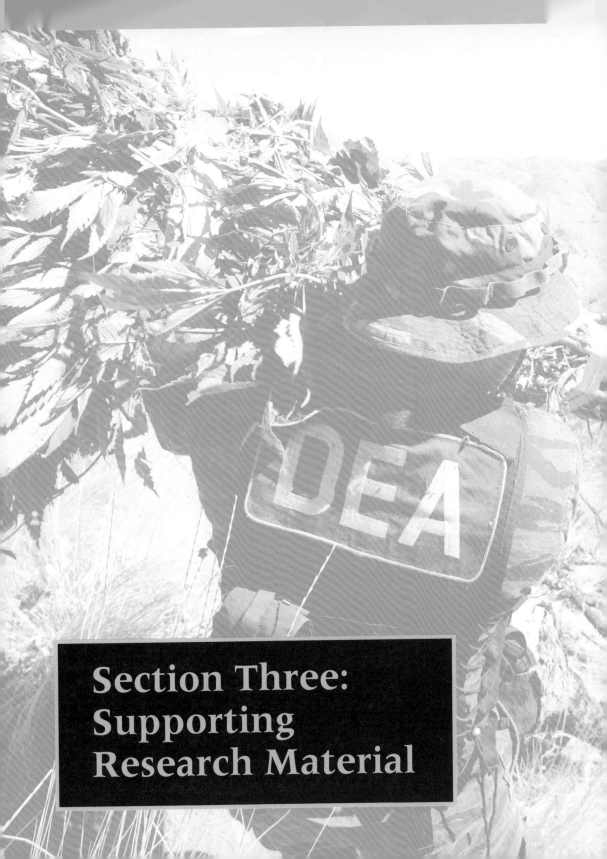

**Section Three:
Supporting
Research Material**

Facts About Marijuana

Editor's Note: These facts can be used in reports or papers to reinforce or add credibility when making important points or claims.

What Is Marijuana?
- Marijuana is a mixture of the dried, shredded leaves, stems, seeds, and flowers of *Cannabis sativa*, the hemp plant.
- The active ingredient in marijuana is delta-9-tetrahydrocannabinol (THC). In the brain, THC connects to cannabinoid receptors on nerve cells and influences their activity.
- A 50 percent concentration of THC can be found in the body—particularly the testes, liver, and brain—up to eight days after using marijuana. Traces of THC can be found in the body up to three months after use.
- Marijuana affects the following parts of the brain:
    1. Cerebellum (responsible for body movement and coordination);
    2. Hippocampus (responsible for learning and memory);
    3. Cerebral cortex (controls higher cognitive functions);
    4. Nucleus accumbens (controls the brain's reward system);
    5. Basal ganglia (controls movement).

- Marijuana is a Schedule I substance under the Controlled Substances Act of 1970. There are five schedules. Schedule I drugs are classified as having a high potential for abuse, no currently accepted medical use, and a lack of accepted safety for use of the drug under medical supervision. Schedule I includes heroin, LSD, and marijuana.

- According to the U.S. Drug Enforcement Agency, average levels of THC (the main active ingredient) in marijuana have risen from less than 1 percent in the mid-1970s to more than 8 percent in 2004.

Marijuana Use in America

- The Office of National Drug Control Policy reports that the most commonly used illegal drugs by those over the age of twelve are:
    Marijuana (12.1 million users, or 5.4 percent of the population);
    Cocaine (1.7 million users, or 0.7 percent of the population);
    Hallucinogens (i.e., LSD, PCP, and ecstasy) (1.3 million users, or 0.6 percent of the population).

According to the 2004 National Survey on Drug Use and Health (NSDUH):

- Approximately 96.8 million Americans ages twelve and older (about 40.2 percent of the population) have reported trying marijuana at least once during their lifetimes.
- Approximately 25.5 million people (10.6 percent of the population) reported past year marijuana use and 14.6 million people (6.1 percent) reported past month marijuana use.
- 3.2 million persons use marijuana on a daily or almost daily basis.
- The number of youths aged twelve to seventeen using marijuana daily or almost daily declined from 358,000 in 2002 to 282,000 in 2003 but increased to 342,000 in 2004.
- According to the Marijuana Policy Project, about six thousand people a day in 2004 used marijuana for the first time—2.1 million Americans.

The National Institute on Drug Abuse reports:

- Marijuana is the most commonly used illegal drug in the United States.

- Nearly 45 percent of U.S. teenagers try marijuana before finishing high school.

Marijuana Crime Statistics

- Of U.S. arrests for marijuana possession, 99 percent are made at the local or state level. Only 1 percent are made by federal authorities.
- From 1972 to 1991 marijuana arrests averaged about 400,000 per year. From 1992 to 2002 marijuana arrests averaged just over 600,000 per year. Since 2002 marijuana arrests have averaged over 700,000 per year.
- In 1991 marijuana arrests accounted for 29 percent of all drug-related arrests; in 2002 marijuana arrests averaged about 46 percent of all drug-related arrests.
- Marijuana possession arrests account for 80 to 90 percent of all marijuana arrests.
- Three out of five people arrested for marijuana possession are under the age of twenty-four.
- Four out of five people arrested for marijuana possession are male. Half of all marijuana possession arrests are males under the age of twenty-four.
- According to the U.S. Bureau of Justice Statistics, more than half (55 percent) of federal prisoners are serving time for a drug offense.
- According to the Federal Bureau of Investigation's Uniform Crime Report, in 2004 39 percent of all drug abuse violations were for marijuana possession.

Marijuana and Abuse

- According to the National Institute on Drug Abuse (NIDA), in 2002 over 280,000 people entering drug treatment programs reported marijuana as their primary drug of abuse.
- The Drug Abuse Warning Network (DAWN) estimated that in 2004 there were more emergency room visits in the United States involving the abuse of prescription drugs than for cocaine, marijuana, or heroin.

- DAWN estimates there were 215,665 emergency room visits relating to marijuana in 2004.
- According to NORML, no one has ever died from an overdose of marijuana.
- The U.S. Substance Abuse and Mental Health Services Administration reports that five substances accounted for 95 percent of all substance abuse treatment admissions in 2004:

  Alcohol (40 percent);

  Opiates, primarily heroin (18 percent);

  Marijuana (16 percent);

  Cocaine (14 percent);

  Stimulants, primarily methamphetamine (8 percent).
- According to the National Survey on Drug Use and Health, students with an average grade of "D" or below were four times as likely to have used marijuana in the past year as students who reported an average grade of "A."
- The U.S. Substance Abuse and Mental Health Services Administration reports that three-quarters of primary marijuana substance abuse treatment admissions were male.

Facts About Medical Marijuana

- Since 1996 eleven states have legalized medical marijuana use: Alaska, Arizona, California, Colorado, Hawaii, Maine, Montana, Nevada, Oregon, Rhode Island, Vermont, and Washington.
- Organizations that have endorsed medical access to marijuana include the Institute of Medicine, the American Academy of Family Physicians, American Bar Association, American Public Health Association, American Society of Addiction Medicine, AIDS Action Council, British Medical Association, California Academy of Family Physicians, California Legislative Council for Older Americans, California Medical Association, California Nurses Association, California

Pharmacists Association, California Society of Addiction Medicine, California-Pacific Annual Conference of the United Methodist Church, Colorado Nurses Association, *Consumer Reports Magazine*, Kaiser Permanente, Lymphoma Foundation of America, Multiple Sclerosis California Action Network, National Association of Attorneys General, National Association of People with AIDS, National Nurses Society on Addictions, New Mexico Nurses Association, New York State Nurses Association, *New England Journal of Medicine*, and Virginia Nurses Association.

- A survey of Californians reports the top three reported uses of medicinal marijuana were for chronic pain (40 percent), AIDS-related (22 percent), and for mood disorders (15 percent).
- According to a November 2004 poll conducted by AARP (American Association of Retired Persons), 72 percent of respondents agreed with the statement, "Adults should be allowed to legally use marijuana for medical purposes if a physician recommends it."
- The British Lung Foundation reports that three to four marijuana cigarettes a day are as dangerous to the lungs as twenty or more tobacco cigarettes a day.
- Marijuana extracts were the first, second, or third most prescribed medicines in the United States each year from 1842 until the 1890s.
- The 1999 U.S. Institute of Medicine (IOM) report, commissioned by the U.S. government, recommended that, under certain narrow conditions, marijuana should be medically available to some patients, even though "numerous studies suggest that marijuana smoke is an important risk factor in the development of respiratory disease."

Finding and Using Sources of Information

No matter what type of essay you are writing, it is necessary to find information to support your point of view. You can use sources such as books, magazine articles, newspaper articles, and online articles.

Using Books and Articles

You can find books and articles in a library by using the library's computer or cataloging system. If you are not sure how to use these resources, ask a librarian to help you. You can also use a computer to find many magazine articles and other articles written specifically for the Internet.

You are likely to find a lot more information than you can possibly use in your essay, so your first task is to narrow it down to what is likely to be most usable. Look at book and article titles. Look at book chapter titles, and examine the book's index to see if it contains information on the specific topic you want to write about. For example, if you want to write about medical marijuana cooperatives and you find a book on marijuana, check the chapter titles and index to be sure it contains information about medical marijuana cooperatives before you bother to check out the book.

For a five-paragraph essay you do not need a great deal of supporting information, so quickly try to narrow down your materials to a few good books and magazine or Internet articles. You do not need dozens. You might even find that one or two good books or articles contain all the information you need.

You probably do not have time to read an entire book, so find the chapters or sections that relate to your topic, and skim these. When you find useful information, copy it onto a notecard or notebook. You should look for supporting facts, statistics, quotations, and examples.

Using the Internet

When you select your supporting information, it is important that you evaluate its source. This is especially important with information you find on the Internet. Because nearly anyone can put information on the Internet, there is as much bad information as good information. Before using Internet information—or any information—try to determine if the source seems to be reliable. Is the author or Internet site sponsored by a legitimate organization? Is it from a government source? Does the author have any special knowledge or training relating to the topic you are looking up? Does the article give any indication of where its information comes from?

Using Your Supporting Information

When you use supporting information from a book, article, interview or other source, there are three important things to remember:

1. *Make it clear whether you are using a direct quotation or a paraphrase.* If you copy information directly from your source, you are quoting it. You must put quotation marks around the information and tell where the information comes from. If you put the information in your own words, you are paraphrasing it.

   Here is an example of using a quotation:
   Drug policy activist Ethan A. Nadelmann refutes claims that marijuana is an addictive, gateway drug that leads to the use of more dangerous illegal drugs. Nadelmann writes, "The vast majority of Americans who have tried marijuana have never gone on to try other illegal drugs, much less get in trouble with them, and most have never even gone on to become regular or problem marijuana users" (29).

Here is an example of a brief paraphrase of the same passage:
Drug policy activist Ethan A. Nadelmann refutes claims that marijuana is an addictive gateway drug that leads to the use of more dangerous illegal drugs. Nadelmann maintains that most Americans who try marijuana do not use it regularly or become problem users and a majority never try other illegal drugs.

2. *Use the information fairly.* Be careful to use supporting information in the way the author intended it. For example, it is unfair to quote an author as saying, "Marijuana is harmless" when he or she intended to say "Many people believe that marijuana is harmless, but frequent use can impair brain activity and motivation." This is called taking information out of context. This is using supporting evidence unfairly.

3. *Give credit where credit is due.* Giving credit is known as citing. You must use citations when you use someone else's information, but not every piece of supporting information needs a citation.

   - If the supporting information is general knowledge—that is, it can be found in many sources—you do not have to cite your source.
   - If you directly quote a source, you must cite it.
   - If you paraphrase information from a specific source, you must cite it.

If you do not use citations where you should, you are *plagiarizing*—or stealing—someone else's work.

Citing Your Sources

There are a number of ways to cite your sources. Your teacher will probably want you to do it in one of three ways:
   - Informal: As in the example in Number 1 above, you tell where you got the information as you present it in the text of your essay.

- Informal list: At the end of your essay, place an unnumbered list of all the sources you used. This tells the reader where, in general, your information came from.
- Formal: A Works Cited list is generally placed at the end of an article or essay, although they may be placed elsewhere depending on your teacher's requirements.

Work Cited

Nadelmann, Ethan A., "An End to Marijuana Prohibition," *National Review* 12 July 2004: 29.

Using MLA Style to Create a Works Cited List

You will probably need to create a list of works cited in your paper. A Works Cited list includes materials that you quoted from, paraphrased, or summarized. When you also include other works you consulted in your research, call this section Works Consulted. There are several different ways to structure these references. The following examples are based on Modern Language Association (MLA) style, one of the major citation styles used by writers.

Book Entries

For most book entries you will need the author's name, the book's title, where it was published, what company published it, and the year it was published. This information is usually found on the inside of the book. Variations on book entries include the following:

A book by a single author:
Guest, Emma. *Children of AIDS: Africa's Orphan Crisis.* London: Sterling, 2003.

Two or more books by the same author:
Friedman, Thomas L. *From Beirut to Jerusalem.* New York: Doubleday, 1989.
---. *The World Is Flat: A Brief History of the Twentieth Century.* New York: Farrar, 2005.

A book by two or more authors:
Pojman, Louis P., and Jeffrey Reiman. *The Death Penalty: For and Against.* Lanham: Rowman, 1998.

A book with an editor:
Friedman, Lauri S., ed. *At Issue: What Motivates Suicide Bombers?* San Diego: Greenhaven, 2004.

Periodical and Newspaper Entries

Entries for sources found in periodicals and newspapers are cited a bit differently from books. For one, these sources usually have a title and a publication name. They also may have specific dates and page numbers. Unlike book entries, you do not need to list where newspapers or periodicals are published or what company publishes them.

An article from a periodical:
> Snow, Keith Harmon. "State Terror in Ethiopia." *Z Magazine* June 2004: 33–35.

An article from a newspaper:
> Constantino, Rebecca. "Fostering Love, Respecting Race." *Los Angeles Times* 14 Dec. 2002: B17.

Internet Sources

To document a source you found online, try to provide as much information on it as possible, including the author's name, the title of the document, date of publication or of last revision, your date of access, and the URL (enclosed in angle brackets).

A Web source:
> Shyovitz, David. "The History and Development of Yiddish." *Jewish Virtual Library* 30 May 2005, accessed 11 Oct 2006 < http://www.jewishvirtual library.org/jsource/History/yiddish.html > .

Your teacher will tell you exactly how information should be cited in your essay. Generally, the very least information needed is the original author's name, the name of the article or other publication, and the URL of the page you are citing.

Be sure you know exactly what information your teacher requires before you start looking for your supporting information so that you know what information to record in your notes.

Sample Essay Topics

Marijuana Is Addictive

Marijuana Is Not Addictive

Marijuana Is a Gateway to the Use of Harder Drugs

Marijuana Is Not a Gateway to the Use of Harder Drugs

The Health Effects of Marijuana

Exploring the Effects of Marijuana on the Human Brain

The Impact of Marijuana on America's Youth

Researchers Should Be Allowed to Obtain Marijuana to Study Its Effects

The History of Marijuana Law

Recreational Marijuana Should Be Legal

Marijuana Should Be Regulated

Marijuana Laws Should Be Reformed

Marijuana Laws Should Not Be Reformed

Penalties for Marijuana Should Be Reduced

Penalties for Marijuana Should Not Be Reduced

The Grassroots Effort to Reform Marijuana Laws

Marijuana and the War on Drugs

Marijuana Should Remain a Schedule I Drug

Marijuana Should Be Rescheduled

The Benefits of Medical Marijuana

The Dangers of Medical Marijuana

Do Medical Marijuana Initiatives Open the Door to Legalization of Marijuana?

States' Rights and Medical Marijuana

Organizations to Contact

American Civil Liberties Union (ACLU)
125 Broad St., 18th Floor, New York, NY 10004-2400 • (212) 549-2500 • e-mail: aclu@aclu.org • Web site: www.aclu.org

The ACLU is a national organization that works to defend Americans' civil rights guaranteed by the U.S. Constitution. It provides legal defense, research, and education. The ACLU opposes the criminal prohibition of marijuana and the resulting civil liberties violations. Its publications include *ACLU Briefing Paper #19: Against Drug Prohibition* and *Ira Glasser on Marijuana Myths and Facts*.

Americans for Safe Access (ASA)
1700 Shattuck Ave., #317, Berkeley, CA 94709 • (888) 929-4367 • e-mail: info@safeaccessnow.org • Web site: www.safeaccessnow.org

ASA is a national grassroots coalition that works with local, state, and national legislators to protect the rights of patients to use and doctors to prescribe marijuana for medical purposes. It provides legal training for lawyers and patients, medical information for doctors and patients, media support for court cases, activist training for grass-roots organizers, and rapid response to law enforcement encounters. ASA publishes *Weekly News Summaries*, which updates subscribers on legal cases and current medical marijuana issues.

Common Sense for Drug Policy
(717) 299-0600 • e-mail: info@csdp.org • Web site: www.csdp.org

Common Sense for Drug Policy is a nonprofit organization dedicated to expanding discussion on drug policy by voicing questions about existing law and educating the public about alternatives to current policies. It offers advice and technical assistance to individuals and organizations working to reform current policies, hosts public forums, and provides pro bono legal assistance to those adversely affected by drug policy. It makes available on its Web site numerous news articles, links, and fact sheets, including "Drug War Facts."

Drug Enforcement Administration (DEA)

Mailstop: AXS, 2401 Jefferson Davis Hwy., Alexandria, VA 22301 • (202) 307-1000 • Web site: www.dea.gov

The DEA is the federal agency charged with enforcing the nation's drug laws. The organization concentrates on stopping the smuggling and distribution of narcotics in the United States and abroad. It publishes the biannual *Microgram Journal* and the monthly *Microgram Bulletins*. Numerous DEA publications are available on its Web site, including *Exposing the Myth of Smoked Medical Marijuana: The Facts and National Drug Threat Assessment 2006*.

Drug Policy Alliance

70 Thirty-sixth St., 16th Floor, New York, NY 10018 • (212) 613-8020 • e-mail: nyc@drugpolicy.org • Web site: www. drugpolicyalliance.com

The alliance, an independent nonprofit organization, supports and publicizes alternatives to current U.S. policies on illegal drugs, including marijuana. To keep Americans informed, the Drug Policy Alliance compiles newspaper articles on drug legalization issues and distributes legislative updates. Its publications include the *Ally* newsletter and the book *It's Just a Plant*.

Marijuana Policy Project

PO Box 77492, Capitol Hill, Washington, DC 20013 • (202) 462-5747 • e-mail: mpp@mpp.org • Web site: www.mpp.org

The Marijuana Policy Project develops and promotes policies to minimize the harm associated with marijuana laws. The project increases public awareness through speaking engagements, educational seminars, and the mass media. Briefing papers, news articles, and the quarterly *MPP Report* can be accessed on its Web site.

National Institute on Drug Abuse (NIDA)

National Institutes of Health, 6001 Executive Blvd., Room 5213, Bethesda, MD 20892 • (301) 443-1124 • e-mail: Information@lists.nida.nih.gov • Web site: www.nida.nih.gov

NIDA supports and conducts research on drug abuse to improve addiction prevention, treatment, and policy efforts. It is dedicated to understanding how drugs of abuse affect the brain and behavior, and it works to rapidly disseminate new information to policy makers, drug abuse counselors, and the general public. It prints the bimonthly *NIDA Notes* newsletter, *NIDA Capsules* fact sheets, and a catalog of research reports and public education materials, such as *Marijuana: Facts for Teens* and *Mind Over Matter*. Some of these materials are available on its Web site.

National Organization for the Reform of Marijuana Laws (NORML)

1600 K St. NW, Suite 501, Washington, DC 20006-2832 • (202) 483-5500 • e-mail: norml@norml.org • Web site: www.norml.org

NORML fights to legalize marijuana and to help those who have been convicted or sentenced for possessing or selling marijuana. It asserts that marijuana can, and should, be used responsibly by adults who so choose. In addition to pamphlets and position papers, NORML publishes weekly press releases, a weekly E-zine, and the *Leaflet* and *Legislative Bulletin* newsletters.

Office of National Drug Control Policy (ONDCP)

Drug Policy Information Clearinghouse, PO Box 6000, Rockville, MD 20849-6000 • (800) 666-3332 • e-mail: ondcp@ncjrs.org • Web site: www.whitehousedrugpolicy.gov

The Office of National Drug Control Policy is responsible for formulating the government's national drug strategy and the president's antidrug policy as well as coordinating the federal agencies responsible for stopping drug trafficking. It has launched drug prevention programs, including the National Youth Anti-Drug Media Campaign, which focuses on the dangers of marijuana. ONDCP publications include *Marijuana Myths & Facts: The Truth Behind 10 Popular Misperceptions*, *What Americans Need to Know About Marijuana*, and *Marijuana Fact Sheet*.

Partnership for a Drug-Free America

405 Lexington Ave., Suite 1601, New York, NY 10174 • (212) 922-1560 • Web site: www.drugfreeamerica.org

The Partnership for a Drug-Free America is a nonprofit organization that utilizes the media to reduce demand for illicit drugs in America. Best known for its national antidrug advertising campaign, the partnership works to educate children about the dangers of drugs and prevent drug use among youths. It produces the *Partnership Newsletter*, annual reports, and monthly press releases about current events with which the partnership is involved.

Bibliography

Books

Booth, Martin, *Cannabis: A History*. New York: Doubleday, 2003. Chronicles the history of marijuana use and prohibition, and prohibition's influence on culture and economics.

Earleywine, Mitchell, *Understanding Marijuana: A New Look at the Scientific Evidence*. New York: Oxford University Press, 2002. Examines the biological, psychological, and societal impact of marijuana and the medical and political debates surrounding its use.

Goodwin, William, *Marijuana*. San Diego, CA: Lucent, 2002. Explores the history of marijuana, its physiological and societal effects, laws regulating its medicinal and recreational uses, and the continuing controversy that surrounds these regulations.

McMahon, George, and Christopher Largen, *Prescription Pot: A Leading Advocate's Heroic Battle to Legalize Medical Marijuana*. Far Hills, NJ: New Horizon, 2003. McMahon, one of the few in the United States who as of 2003 could smoke marijuana legally, campaigns for the legalization of medical marijuana. The book documents his conversations with legislators, law-enforcement personnel, and other medical marijuana users, legal and not.

McMullin, Jordan, ed., *Marijuana*. San Diego, CA: Greenhaven, 2005. Looks at the history of marijuana, including its introduction into Europe in the nineteenth century, the controversy over its use in the United States in the 1960s and the 1970s, and the current debate over its legalization and medical properties.

Periodicals

Cohen, Harold E., "A Closer Look at Marijuana," *Drug Topics*, December 8, 2003.

Conant, Marcus, "Medical Marijuana," *Family Practice News,* July 1, 2005.

Drug Enforcement Agency, "Exposing the Myth of Medical Marijuana," www.usdoj.gov/dea.

Feran, Tom, "Ruling on Marijuana Really Is Just a Sick Joke," *Cleveland Plain Dealer,* June 10, 2005.

Friedman, Milton, "Weed All About It; Yes, I Think We Should Legalize Marijuana—and Maybe All Drugs. But the Big News Is That Some Prominent Conservative Republicans Agree with Me," *Texas Monthly,* July 2005.

Grinspoon, Lester S., "A Cannabis Odyssey," *Harvard Crimson,* September 15, 2003.

Harvard Health Letter, "Reefer Rx: Marijuana as Medicine," September 2004.

Issues & Controversies on File, "Medical Marijuana Update," July 8, 2005.

Marijuana Policy Project, "Medical Marijuana Briefing Paper," 2006. www.mpp.org.

Marshall, Patrick, "Marijuana Laws," *CQ Researcher,* February 11, 2005.

National Institute on Drug Abuse, "Marijuana Abuse," *NIDA Research Report Series,* July 2005.

New York Times, "When Medical Marijuna Is Misused," June 24, 2005.

Office of National Drug Control Policy, "Marijuana," *Drug Facts,* February 27, 2006. www.whitehousedrug policy.gov.

San Francisco Chronicle, "Marijuana Madness," December 29, 2005.

Talvi, Silja J.A., "Reefer Madness, Redux," *Nation,* April 9, 2003.

Tierney, John, "Marijuana Pipe Dreams," *New York Times,* August 27, 2005.

Web Sites

Drug War Facts (www.drugwarfacts.org). Sponsored by Common Sense for Drug Policy, this site provides facts and statistics about marijuana and publishes quotes from a variety of sources concerning marijuana and marijuana law in support of the position that marijuana policies should be reformed.

The Facts About Marijuana (www.marijuana-info.org). Sponsored by the National Institute on Drug Abuse (NIDA), the site provides fact sheets, reports, and links to NIDA articles in support of the position that marijuana is a dangerous drug.

Marijuana.com (www.marijuana.com). Offers a wide variety of information favoring the medicinal and recreational use of marijuana, including fact sheets, articles, and reports.

Medical Marijuana ProCon.org (www.medicalmarijuana procon.org). Publishes views on both sides of the medical-marijuana debate in answer to a wide variety of questions from the general to the specific, including, does marijuana have medical value and can marijuana help Alzheimer's disease?

Index

Picture Credits

Cover: AP/Wide World Photo
© Bettmann/CORBIS, 24
© Joao Luiz Bulcao/CORBIS, 51
© The Cover Story/CORBIS, 38
© Henry Diltz/CORBIS, 27
© Jim Young/Reuters/CORBIS, 32
Steve Zmina, 12, 19, 25, 34, 47

About the Editor

Louise Gerdes earned a bachelor's degree in psychology from the University of California, Berkeley, a master's in literature and writing from California State University, San Marcos, and a Juris Doctor from the University of Florida College of Law. Currently, she teaches composition, speech, and critical thinking at the University of Phoenix and develops curriculum for online college courses. She lives in Vista, California, with her tuxedo cat Phineas.